SPANISH II
UNIT FOUR

CONTENTS

I. **CLOTHES, CLOTHING** 2

    Listening Exercises I 25

II. **GRAMMAR: THE POSSESSIVE** 31

    Listening Exercises II 51

III. **GRAMMAR: THE PRESENT PARTICIPLE** 56

    Listening Exercises III 66

IV. **GRAMMAR REVIEW: UNIT THREE** 69

V. **CULTURE: SPAIN** 77

    VOCABULARY LIST 82

Author:	**Katherine Engle, M.A.**
Managing Editor:	Alan Christopherson, M.S.
Revision Editor:	Christine E. Wilson, B.A., M.A.
Illustrators:	Steve Ring
	Kyle Bennett
Graphic Designer:	Dawn Tessier

804 N. 2nd Ave. E., Rock Rapids, IA 51246-1759
© MMI by Alpha Omega Publications, Inc.   All rights reserved.
LIFEPAC is a registered trademark of Alpha Omega Publications, Inc.

All trademarks and/or service marks referenced in this material are the property of their respective owners. Alpha Omega Publications, Inc. makes no claim of ownership to any trademarks and/or service marks other than their own and their affiliates', and makes no claim of affiliation to any companies whose trademarks may be listed in this material, other than their own.

SPANISH II: UNIT FOUR
INTRODUCTION

Clothing is often one of the first units taught in a foreign language. The ability to differentiate people by wardrobe is useful when communicating with native speakers.

Picture yourself lost in a public situation (the park, a museum), separated from your companion. The first information you would provide a policeman is what that companion is wearing. Likewise, you may find yourself helping out a native speaker in a crowded place someday. For the sake of precision, the vocabulary is expanded to include related descriptive information about clothing.

Expressing possession in Spanish is covered in the grammar sections. You should be able to use all **four** means of possession (the possessive pronoun, etc.) to sound more natural and less "English."

You will continue to practice the correct usage of "for," "because," and "but," as well as learn more about the use of the gerund. Knowledge of these structures enables you to create longer sentences of more varied structure. Your Spanish will become more interesting and pleasant to listen to and read.

Finally, you will be interested to learn of Spain's vast linguistic and provincial divisions. There are fourteen different languages spoken in Spain. Five of the most commonly spoken will be identified, and you will learn where these languages are spoken on the Iberian Peninsula. These languages are dispersed among the fifteen major provinces of Spain.

OBJECTIVES

Read these objectives. When you have finished this Unit, you should be able to do the following:

1. Identify items of clothing.
2. Describe clothing by age, color, and condition.
3. Use four different expressions of possession, including adjectives and pronouns.
4. Use the gerund, or its equivalent, in Spanish sentences.
5. Differentiate the need for the gerund/present participle and the infinitive in Spanish sentences.
6. Describe the geography of Spain.
7. Identify the major provincial divisions of Spain.
8. Identify the major linguistic divisions of Spain.

I. CLOTHES, CLOTHING

LA ROPA PARA EL TRABAJO

A. Ofrecemos los pantalones formales para el trabajo. Se vende pantalones negros y de color café. Hay las tallas desde 28 hasta 44. $50.00

B. Escoja los pantalones con una chaqueta cuando necesita un traje para la oficina. Puede comprar una chaqueta del mismo color que el pantalón. Hay las tallas desde 28 hasta 44. $75.00

C. Para completar su traje, escoja una camisa fina. Se venden camisas azules, blancas, de color café, amarillas y verdes. Las tallas son S, M, L, XL y XXL. $32.00

D. Escoja una corbata de seda (of silk). Hay varios colores y estilos. $25.00

E. Vendemos las blusas de varios colores para aumentar su colección. Son de una tela (fabric) suave y fácil a cuidar. Hay las tallas desde 2 hasta 18. $25.00.

F. La mujer profesional puede comprar una falda para el trabajo. Se ve la falda larga, pero también la ofrecemos en mediana. Es bueno comprar una falda de cada uno de los cuatro colores: azul, café, blanco y negro. Hay las tallas desde 2 hasta 18. $45.00

G. Para hacer un traje, escoja una chaqueta a $45.00.

H. Los vestidos que ofrecemos son apropiados para el trabajo. Hay las tallas desde 2 hasta 18. Precios a partir de $40.00.

LA ROPA DEPORTIVA

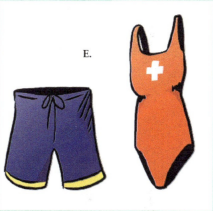

A. Para un picnic o un partido de fútbol los pantalones cortos (el short) son perfectos. Se venden de varios colores para damas y caballeros. Hay las tallas S, M, L y XL para damas y desde 28 hasta 44 para caballeros. $10.00

B. Tenemos camisetas de una variedad de colores. Compre dos o tres para su tiempo deportivo. Hay las tallas S, M, L y XL para damas y caballeros. $15.00

C. Todo el mundo lleva los jeans (los vaqueros). Los nuestros son de la calidad más alta. Hay las tallas desde 2 hasta 18 para mujeres y de 28 hasta 44 para caballeros. Precios a partir de $15.00.

D. Cuando hace fresco, escoja una chaqueta sudadera. Tenemos las tallas S, M, L y XL para damas y caballeros. $20.00

E. ¿Va Ud. de vacaciones? Tenemos los trajes de baño para damas y caballeros. Se venden las tallas S, M, L y XL. Compre dos para la playa a estos precios baratos. $25.00

Match the Spanish terms to the English.

1.1
1. _____ la chaqueta
2. _____ los jeans
3. _____ los pantalones
4. _____ la camiseta
5. _____ la falda
6. _____ la camisa
7. _____ la blusa
8. _____ la corbata
9. _____ los caballeros
10. _____ el traje
11. _____ las damas
12. _____ los pantalones cortos
13. _____ la ropa
14. _____ el vestido

a. the gentlemen
b. the jacket (dress or casual)
c. the suit
d. the shirt (button-down)
e. the clothing
f. the ladies
g. the jeans
h. the tie
i. the pants (men's or women's)
j. the blouse
k. the shorts
l. the T-shirt
m. the skirt
n. the dress

 Adult check _____
                              Initial   Date

LOS COMPLEMENTOS

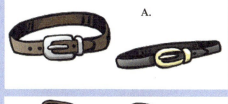
A.

B.

C.

D.

E.

F.

G.

H.

I.

Ya sabemos que Ud. quiere hacer las compras fácilmente. Por eso vendemos una selección completa de complementos.

A. Los cinturones de cuero de alta calidad son para damas y caballeros. $20.00

B. Tenemos bolsas elegantes importadas de Italia. Escoja el color olivo, azul o café. $50.00

C. ¿Necesita guantes? Los vendemos de cuero suave para damas y caballeros. $20.00

D. Se venden billeteras y carteras para su dinero, fotos y tarjetas de crédito. Tienen bolsillos adentro y se cierran seguramente. $20.00.

E. F. Vendemos zapatos de cuero fino. Hay zapatos de tacones altos (E) o zapatos de tacones bajos (F) para damas. Serán cómodos para el trabajo o los fines de semana. Hay zapatos negros y de color café. $25.00

G. También hay zapatos negros y de color café para caballeros en estilos diferentes. $65.00

H, I. Compre un par de botas de cuero fino de la Argentina. Las tenemos para damas y caballeros del número 6 hasta 12 incluso las anchas y estrechas. $50.00

Use the visual and textual cues provided to summarize this new vocabulary. Write the appropriate English term next to each Spanish word.

1.2
a. la billetera _____
b. los zapatos _____
c. los guantes _____
d. un par _____
e. la bolsa _____
f. los zapatos de tacones altos _____
g. el cinturón _____
h. ancho(a) _____
i. estrecho(a) _____
j. las botas _____
k. los zapatos de tacones bajos _____

Fill in the blanks with the correct Spanish vocabulary term.

1.3
1. Where is my *wallet*?

   ¿Dónde está mi _____ ?

2. Don't wear brown *shoes* with *a* black *suit*.

   No lleves _____ de color café con _____ negro.

3. I'm wearing *jeans* and *a T-shirt* to the party.

   Yo llevo _____ y _____ a la fiesta.

4. It's cold. You can't wear *shorts*.

   Hace frío. No puedes llevar _____ .

5. Carmen is buying *a purse* that looks good with her *high heels*.

   Carmen compra _____ que hace juego (matches) con sus _____ .

6. He needs to wear *a suit* and *a tie* to the office.

   Él necesita llevar _____ y _____ a la oficina.

7. That *skirt* doesn't need *a belt*.

   Esa _____ no requiere _____ .

8. They need *some blouses*.

   Ellas necesitan _____ .

9. My dad has to wear *wide shoes*.

   Mi padre tiene que llevar _____ .

10. I'm looking for *men's clothing* (clothing for men).

    Busco _____ para _____ .

✓ Adult check _____
                       Initial   Date

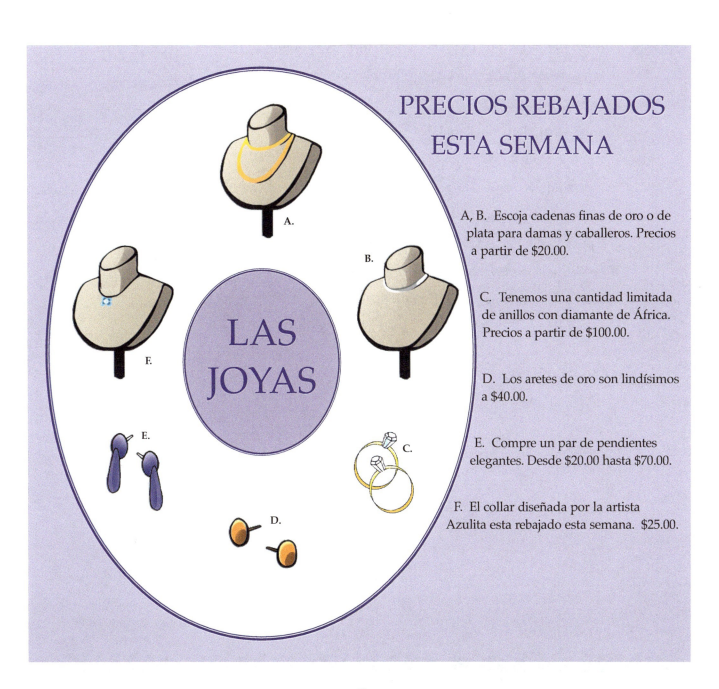

PRECIOS REBAJADOS ESTA SEMANA

LAS JOYAS

A, B. Escoja cadenas finas de oro o de plata para damas y caballeros. Precios a partir de $20.00.

C. Tenemos una cantidad limitada de anillos con diamante de África. Precios a partir de $100.00.

D. Los aretes de oro son lindísimos a $40.00.

E. Compre un par de pendientes elegantes. Desde $20.00 hasta $70.00.

F. El collar diseñada por la artista Azulita esta rebajado esta semana. $25.00.

Practice this group of terms by completing the matching exercise. Write the correct letter answer on the line

1.4
1. _____ la cadena de oro   a. the necklace
2. _____ el arete   b. the gold chain
3. _____ el collar   c. the ring
4. _____ la cadena   d. the (post) earring
5. _____ la cadena de plata   e. the drop earring
6. _____ el anillo   f. the chain
7. _____ el pendiente   g. the silver chain

Answer the following questions about the new vocabulary.

1.5
a. Is *la ropa deportiva* meant to be worn for play or for formal occasions? _____
b. What are *las joyas*? _____
c. *Cuero* is what kind of material? _____
d. If *la talla* is offered in S, M, or L, how would you define *la talla*? _____
e. How would you express *los complementos* in English? _____
f. Under what section would you look for clothes for work? _____
g. If *el precio* is offered as $55.00, how would you define *el precio*? _____
h. If *los deportes* are *sports*, how would you define *deportivo*? _____
i. Should you wear *la ropa deportiva* to something *informal*? _____
j. On what part of the body are *las cadenas* usually found? _____

Continue reading the catalog:

LOS ARTÍCULOS PERSONALES

A. La ropa interior para damas
B. La ropa interior para caballeros
C. Los calcetines

D. Las medias
E. Los pijamas
F. Los zapatillos

LOS COMPLEMENTOS

Para estar de moda necesita escoger bien.

A. Se venden las mochilas diseñadas por Azulita. $15.00

B. Escoja una bufanda elegante para su traje. $20.00

C. Compre sombreros para toda su familia. Precios a partir de $15.00.

D. Hay gorras deportivas de los colores de su equipo favorito. $10.00

E. Cuando llueve, necesita un impermeable y un paraguas duradero. $15.00

¡**Felicidades!** Congratulations! You have completed the introduction to new vocabulary.

 Summarize all you have read by labeling each picture with the correct Spanish term. Include the correct article *el*, *la*, *los*, or *las*.

1.6

a. _____   b. _____   c. _____   d. _____

e. _____   f. _____   g. _____   h. _____

i. _____   j. _____   k. _____   l. _____

m. _____   n. _____   o. _____   p. _____

q. _____   r. _____   s. _____   t. _____

u. _____   v. _____   w. _____   x. _____

y. _____   z. _____   aa. _____   bb. _____

cc. _____   dd. _____   ee. _____   ff. _____

Determine the meaning of the italicized words. Study the accompanying drawing and circle the appropriate translation.

1.7

a. El collar es *caro*.
The necklace is (long, cheap, expensive).

b. La camisa es *fea*.
The shirt is (cheap, ugly, elegant).

c. El vestido es *elegante*.
The dress is (casual, elegant, wrinkled).

d. Los tenis están *sucios*.
The sneakers are (dirty, old, clean).

e. Los zapatos de tacones altos son *estrechos*. The high heels are (wide, new, narrow).

f. La camiseta es *barata*.
The T-shirt is (cheap, clean, expensive).

g. La blusa es *bonita*.
The blouse is (ugly, pretty, cheap).

h. La camiseta es azul *claro*. The T-shirt is (dark, light) blue.

i. La ropa es *informal*.
The clothing is (formal, new, casual).

j. Los pantalones están *arrugados*.
The pants are (elegant, wrinkled, casual).

k. La camisa está *limpia*.
The shirt is (clean, dirty, old).

l. El traje de baño es azul *oscuro*.
The bathing suit is (light, dark) blue.

m. Los zapatos son *anchos*.
The shoes are (clean, wide, narrow).

n. Los pantalones son *cortos*.
The pants are (short, long, clean).

o. La gorra es *nueva*.
The cap is (old, dirty, new).

p. El vestido es *largo*.
The dress is (wide, long, short).

q. La chaqueta es *floja*.
The jacket is (loose, expensive, tight).

r. La ropa es *vieja*.
The clothing is (new, casual, old).

s. Los zapatos son *apretados*.
The shoes are (cheap, tight, loose).

t. El traje es *fino*.
The suit is (ugly, casual, fine).

Summarize the vocabulary by giving the English for the following words.

1.8
a. ancho(a) _____
b. apretado(a) _____
c. arrugado(a) _____
d. barato(a) _____
e. caro(a) _____
f. informal _____
g. corto(a) _____
h. elegante _____
i. estrecho(a) _____
j. feo(a) _____
k. fino(a) _____
l. flojo(a) _____
m. bonito(a) _____
n. largo(a) _____
o. claro(a) _____
p. limpio(a) _____
q. nuevo(a) _____
r. oscuro(a) _____
s. sucio(a) _____
t. viejo(a) _____

SUPPLEMENTAL VOCABULARY

bastante – rather, very, quite, enough
comprar – to buy
conseguir (e-i) – to get
deber – to owe; should, must
llevar – to wear, carry
muy – very
obtener – to get, obtain

probarse (o-ue) – to try on
tan – so (+ adjective)
tener – to have
tener que + infinitive – to have to, must
traer – to bring
vestirse – to get dressed

Create a set of flashcards to help you review easily and quickly.

1.9 Write the English translation of each vocabulary word on one side of an index card. On the other side, write the Spanish term. Review the vocabulary daily for about 10 minutes, using these cards.

✓ Adult check _____
                      Initial   Date

Read the following passage out loud, filling in a Spanish term (and its definite or indefinite article when needed) for each drawing. Practice to see how quickly and accurately you can complete the stories.

1.10

a. Acabo de asistir a una boda. Me visto de _____ amarillo. Llevé _____ azules y _____ azul. Era muy elegante. Pero mi novio llevó _____ y _____ vieja y fea.

b. Mi padre trabaja en una oficina muy importante. Siempre se viste muy bien para el trabajo. Lleva _____, _____ y _____ todos los días. Sus _____ siempre están muy limpios. Cuando hace frío, lleva _____ también.

c. Alonso es muy deportivo. Para el campeonato, lleva _____ y _____ negra. Sus _____ son negros también. Prefiere llevar _____ para guardar del sol. Para los pies tiene que llevar _____.

d. Voy de vacaciones. Traigo la ropa informal. Hago la maleta con _____, dos _____ y dos _____. No necesito ni _____ ni _____. ¡Cuánto me alegro!

e. Pasé un día difícil. Llovía y no tenía _____. Dejé _____ en casa también. No me gusta lleva _____, y por eso mi _____ ahora están llenos de agua. Tenía que llevar _____ mojado (wet) por toda la mañana.

✓ Adult check _____
                      Initial   Date

Create Venn diagrams. Think of three items for each separate category and two that fit into the blended area in the middle. Color your diagrams. Make each circle of each diagram a different color so that the blended area in the middle stands out.

Example: ___los zapatos___

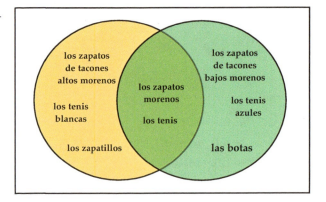

1.11

_____

_____

 Adult check _____
                                    Initial   Date

Fill in the blanks with the appropriate translation of the italicized words.

1.12
1. She wore *a beautiful dress* and *high heels* to the dance.

   Llevó _____ hermoso y _____ al baile.

2. Where are Juan's *socks*?

   ¿Dónde están los _____ de Juan?

3. *Jeans* and *a T-shirt* are good for class.

   _____ y _____ son buenos para la clase.

4. He took off *his hat** and *jacket* and put on *a sweater*.

   Se quitó _____ y _____ y se puso _____ .

5. I bought *an expensive wallet* for my father and *a backpack* for my sister.

   Compré _____ para mi papá y _____ para mi hermana.

6. It's raining. You need *an umbrella* or *a raincoat*.

   Llueve. Necesita _____ y _____ .

7. For work, you *must* wear *a suit*.

   Para el trabajo, Ud. _____ llevar _____ .

8. The pants are *wrinkled* and *dirty*.

   Los pantalones están _____ y _____ .

9. She needs *a new skirt*.

   Necesita _____ .

10. Whose *light* brown *blouse* is this?

    ¿De quién es esta _____ de color café _____ ?

***Note:** In Spanish, use the definite article rather than the possessive adjective before articles of clothing owned by the subject of the sentence.

 Study the picture of Martín's very messy room. Answer the following questions about the picture in complete Spanish sentences.

1.13 a. ¿Es la almohada blanca?

b. ¿Es el libro verde?

c. ¿Qué cuelga de la puerta?

d. ¿Hay una camiseta púrpura sobre la mesa de noche? ¿De qué colores son?

e. ¿Dónde están los tenis?

f. ¿De qué color son los jeans? En qué condición están?

g. ¿Qué ropa está sobre la almohada de la cama?

h. ¿Es el calcetín sobre la lámpara de color café?

i. ¿De qué colores es la gorra?

j. ¿Qué ropa está limpia?

Read the five descriptions. Draw and dress a figure according to each description given. Pay attention to the color of the clothing as well.

1.14

a. Ella lleva una falda púrpura y una blusa negra. Lleva también calcetines verdes y zapatos de tacones altos.

b. Él lleva vaqueros. Sus tenis son rojos. Su camiseta es azul claro. Lleva también una gorra roja.

c. Él lleva pantalones negros y una camisa blanca. Lleva también una corbata roja, verde y anaranjada.

d. Ella lleva una chaqueta y un sombrero azul. Sus pantalones son de color café oscuro. Lleva botas también.

e. Ella es muy elegante. Tiene un vestido largo. Es amarillo. Lleva un collar caro. Sus pendientes son muy grandes. Sus zapatos de tacones bajos son negros.

✔ Adult check _____
                    Initial   Date

Look over the characters below. On the lines provided, write four complete sentences describing what each person is wearing. Use at least four new vocabulary terms for each description. Watch out for gender and number agreement.

1.15

a. _____

b. _____

c. _____

d. _____

18

e. _____
_____
_____
_____
_____

✔ Adult check _____
                    Initial   Date

Decide where each person is going tonight. Write three suggestions for clothing appropriate to the destination or occasion after the phrase *debe llevar*. Include descriptive terms such as "dirty," "long," "blue," etc., for each suggestion. Write three suggestions as to what he/she shouldn't wear after the phrase *no debe llevar*, using descriptive terms also. Use complete Spanish sentences.

1.16

1. Rafael trabaja para una compañía de construcción. Va al sitio (site) de trabajo a las siete de la mañana.

    Debe llevar _____.

    No debe llevar _____.

2. Paco asiste a una conferencia profesional para médicos. Tiene lugar (It takes place) en un hotel elegante.

    Debe llevar _____.

    No debe llevar _____.

3. Elisa va a la boda *(wedding)* de su prima. Es el veinte de diciembre por la noche.

    Debe llevar _____.

    No debe llevar _____.

4. Cristina y su amiga van a la playa el sábado. Va a hacer mucho calor.

   Deben llevar _____.

   No deben llevar _____.

5. Jesús necesita visitar la biblioteca para estudiar con un amigo.

   Debe llevar _____.

   No debe llevar _____.

6. Carmen y yo trabajamos para una compañía internacional.

   Debemos llevar _____.

   No debemos llevar _____.

7. Yo asisto a una reunión informal después de las clases.

   Debo llevar _____.

   No debo llevar _____.

8. Mis amigos van a una fiesta de cumpleaños a la casa de Chamo.

   Deben llevar _____.

   No deben llevar _____.

✓ Adult check _____
                    Initial   Date

Matching. Match English to the Spanish terms in *Parte 1* and Spanish to the English terms in *Parte 2*.

1.17

Parte 1

1. _____ los pantalones   a. the stockings
2. _____ el vestido   b. the pants
3. _____ la corbata   c. the backpack
4. _____ los calcetines   d. the jacket
5. _____ la chaqueta   e. the size
6. _____ las medias   f. the dress
7. _____ los pijamas   g. the bracelet
8. _____ la talla   h. the tie
9. _____ la pulsera   i. the pajamas
10. _____ la mochila   j. the socks

Parte 2

1.	_____	clean	a.	fino
2.	_____	the umbrella	b.	apretado
3.	_____	light (color)	c.	limpio
4.	_____	tight	d.	probarse
5.	_____	the scarf	e.	los guantes
6.	_____	the skirt	f.	el paraguas
7.	_____	fine	g.	la bufanda
8.	_____	to try on	h.	claro
9.	_____	the gloves	i.	muy
10.	_____	very	j.	la falda

Translate the following sentences into the opposite language.

1.18

a. El hombre se viste de un traje nuevo con una camisa blanca.

_____

b. Me pongo una falda larga, pero es apretada.

_____

c. Tengo una blusa azul claro que llevo con pantalones blancos.

_____

d. Ella compró unas botas feas.

_____

e. Llevamos zapatos de tacones altos con un vestido formal.

_____

f. Traigo un paraguas viejo.

_____

g. Ella siempre lleva muchas joyas.

_____

h. Los pantalones cortos con una camiseta y una gorra son buenos para el picnic.

_____

i. Recibo pendientes elegantes para mi cumpleaños.

j. El traje fino es muy elegante para él.

k. She is wearing an old skirt with *(con)* a black blouse.

l. Do you have a clean shirt?

m. Cristina bought an elegant necklace.

n. The boy's boots are very tight.

o. Jorge got a new backpack and a new wallet.

p. He wears a fine tie with his formal suit.

q. The gold chain is rather long.

r. Jeans are very casual for work.

s. The cheap shoes are ugly.

t. Carlos brings an umbrella and a raincoat to school.

Speaking

Marisol and Jaime are discussing what to wear to a cousin's wedding this afternoon. Using the model below, write a dialogue with a learning partner. Present the dialogue to your class.

1.19

Parte 1   **Marisol**   **Jaime**

Marisol: We are going to have fun *(divertirnos)* this afternoon. I like to see what everyone is wearing.

Jaime: I want to go to the wedding *(la boda)*, but I don't like formal clothing.

Marisol: I bought a new, elegant dress. It's dark green.

Jaime: Don't forget *(No te olvides de)* to wear shoes!

Marisol: Very funny *(divertido)*. I have black high heels.

Jaime: Well, I'm going to wear jeans, a shirt, and my red sneakers.

Marisol: What? A wedding is a formal occasion!

Jaime: I don't care *(No me importa)*. I don't like to wear a new suit.

Marisol: You have to wear a shirt and a tie! And pants, too. Jeans are too casual.

Jaime: I don't have a dark-colored jacket to wear with my blue pants.

a. _____   _____

b. _____   _____

c. _____   _____

d. _____   _____

e. _____   _____

Parte 2   **Marisol**   **Jaime**

> You don't have to wear a jacket. Do you have a good (*fina*) tie?

> I can wear my red tie with my red sneakers!

> No, no, no. You have dark shoes, don't you?

> I have black shoes.

> OK. You can wear the blue pants with a blue shirt, the red tie, and the black shoes.

> Thanks for the help, I don't like formal clothing.

> You're welcome. You must trust me (*Hay que confiar en mí*). You don't have to be elegant, but need to dress well.

f. _____   _____

g. _____   _____

h. _____   _____

i. _____

✓ Adult check _____
                    Initial   Date

Write a composition about your wardrobe. Write 10 (ten) complete Spanish sentences. Start by describing what you wore to a particular formal occasion. Use the preterit tense. Continue with today's outfit, using the present tense. End your composition by describing what you are going to wear this weekend (use the construction *ir + a +* infinitive to describe the future).

1.20

✔ Adult check _____
                       Initial   Date

🟡 LISTENING EXERCISES I 🟡

Exercise 1. You will hear a question about each drawing. Decide if that sentence accurately describes the drawing. If it is accurate, write an agreeing sentence. If not, correct the sentence you heard by identifying the drawing accurately. [CD–C, Track 1]

Example:

¿Es una bufanda?

No, es una gorra.

¿Es una falda?

Sí, es una falda.

1. _____ 2. _____

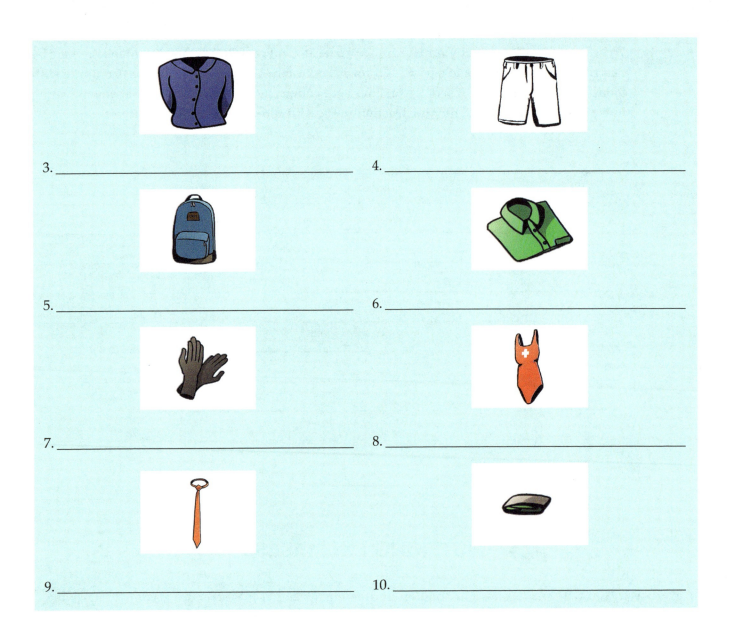

3. _____ 4. _____

5. _____ 6. _____

7. _____ 8. _____

9. _____ 10. _____

Exercise 2. Look at each illustration as you listen to a description of it. Decide which items of clothing are mentioned in each description. Complete the sentences according to the drawings and the descriptions. [CD–C, Track 2]

1. Lleva la ropa…
   a. formal.
   b. informal.
   c. sucia.

2. El vestido es…
   a. de tacones bajos.
   b. bajo.
   c. largo.

3. En el jardín lleva…
   a. un short.
   b. guantes.
   c. calcetines negros.

4. La bolsa es…
   a. roja.
   b. azul.
   c. negra.

5. A la playa llevan…
   a. zapatos elegantes.
   b. una gorra.
   c. una camiseta.

Exercise 3. Look over the drawings below. As you listen to each description, decide which person is being described. Write the number of your choice in the blank. [CD–C, Track 3]

a. _____

b. _____

c. _____

d. _____

e. _____

Review the material in this section in preparation for the Self Test. The Self Test will check your mastery of this particular section. The items missed on this Self Test will indicate specific areas where restudy is needed for mastery.

SELF TEST 1

1.01 Describe the appropriate clothing, for your area, for each month listed. Express yourself in complete Spanish sentences. Include at least *three* different articles of clothing for each month. (2 pts. each)

a. En julio las personas _____

b. En diciembre yo _____

c. En octubre mi familia _____

d. En marzo los estudiantes _____

e. En abril mis amigos y yo _____

1.02 Identify each item of clothing or accessory in Spanish. Include the definite or indefinite article with each answer. (1 pt. each)

a. _____

b. _____ c. _____ d. _____

e. _____ f. _____ g. _____

h. _____ i. _____ j. _____

28

1.03   **Choose and circle the appropriate adjective in order to complete the descriptions accurately.**
(1 pt. each)

 a. Los calcetines están (sucios / limpios).

 f. La camiseta es (apretada / floja).

 b. Los zapatos son (viejos / nuevos).

 g. La bufanda es (azul / de color café).

 c. El collar es (barato / caro).

 h. El traje (está arrugado / es fino).

 d. La corbata es (estrecha / ancha).

 i. El vestido es (informal / elegante).

 e. La falda es (verde / roja).

 j. Los pantalones son (largos / cortos).

1.04   **Translate the phrases into Spanish.** (2 pts. each)

a.   a new hat   _____

b.   a fine dress   _____

c.   a wrinkled shirt   _____

d.   the casual clothing   _____

e.   some long pants   _____

f.   some tight shoes   _____

g.   an ugly tie   _____

h.   an expensive bracelet   _____

i.   a formal suit   _____

j.   a dirty skirt   _____

1.05 **Is this clothing suitable for the occasion? If your answer is no, make an appropriate suggestion in Spanish.** (2 pts. each)

a. un partido de béisbol: un vestido elegante _____

b. la iglesia: la camisa limpia y una corbata _____

c. la casa: los pijamas _____

d. la playa: las botas y un suéter _____

e. una fiesta formal: los jeans y una camiseta _____

f. el trabajo en una oficina: el traje de baño _____

g. el supermercado: un short y los tenis _____

h. el teatro: una falda y una blusa fina _____

i. una clase de la universidad: muchas joyas _____

j. el cine: la ropa informal _____

1.06 **Decide what item of clothing is most logical for each part of the body. Write your choice in the space provided, using the definite or indefinite article.** (1 pt. each)

a. _____ b. _____ c. _____ d. _____ e. _____

f. _____ g. _____ h. _____ i. _____ j. _____

64 / 80

Score _____
Adult check _____
Initial   Date

II. GRAMMAR: THE POSSESSIVE

There are many ways to express possession in Spanish. Read the following sample sentences.

Es el vestido de Elena.	It's Elena's dress.
Es el vestido de ella.	It's her dress (the dress of her).
Es su vestido.	It's her dress.
Es el vestido suyo.	It's HER dress.
Es suyo.	It's hers.

Answer the question.

2.1 Why is *suyo* masculine, if it translates as *her*? Does *suyo* agree in number and gender with *Elena* or *vestido*?

_____

What you should notice right away is the lack of the *apostrophe + s* ('s). This type of grammatical construction does NOT exist in the Spanish language. Rather, word order and special adjectives and pronouns are used to show possession. Read the following sample sentences.

Es la casa de Pedro.	It's Pedro's house.
Es la casa de él.	It's his house (the house of him).
Es su casa.	It's his house.
Es la casa suya.	It's HIS house.
Es suya.	It's his.

Translate this group of sentences and answer the question.

2.2 a. Son los tenis de Raúl. _____

b. Son los tenis de él. _____

c. Son sus tenis. _____

d. Son los tenis suyos. _____

e. Son suyos. _____

f. If Raúl is one person, why is *suyos* used? _____

As you learned in Spanish I, possessive adjectives and pronouns agree in meaning with the owner **but** in number and gender with the object owned.

You will notice we have expressed Raúl's ownership of the sneakers by his name, by possessive adjectives, and by pronouns. Review the parts of speech used previously:

> Son los **tenis de Raúl**. (noun + **de** + noun)
> Son los **tenis de él**. (noun + **de** + pronoun)
> Son **sus** tenis. (possessive adjective)
> Son los tenis **suyos**. (stressed possessive adjective)
> Son **suyos**. (possessive pronoun)

Translate the following sentences.

2.3 a. Es la falda de mí. _____
   b. Es mi falda. _____
   c. Es la falda mía. _____
   d. Es mía. _____
   e. Es la ropa de Ricardo y yo. _____
   f. Es la ropa de nosotros. _____
   g. Es nuestra ropa. _____
   h. Es la ropa nuestra. _____
   i. Es nuestra. _____
   j. Son los guantes de ti. _____
   k. Son tus guantes. _____
   l. Son los guantes tuyos. _____
   m. Son tuyos. _____

At this point, you can see the pattern established by the text.

Following that pattern, express each person's ownership by filling in the correct possessive terms.

2.4
   La camisa/Carmen

   a. It's Carmen's shirt. Es _____ de _____ .
   b. It's her shirt. Es _____ de _____ .
   c. It's her shirt. Es _____ camisa.
   d. It's HER shirt. Es _____ camisa _____ .
   e. It's hers. Es _____ .

Did you remember to make your possessive forms agree in number and gender with *camisa*?

Express each person's ownership by filling in the correct possessive forms.

2.5 Los pendientes / mis hermanas

a. They're my sisters' earrings. Son _____ de _____ .

b. They're their earrings. Son _____ de ellas.

c. They're their earrings. Son _____ pendientes.

d. They're THEIR earrings. Son _____ pendientes _____ .

e. They're theirs. Son _____ .

Remember, the possessive terms should agree in number and gender with the earrings!

Las medias / mi madre

f. They're my mother's stockings. Son _____ de _____ .

g. They're her stockings. Son _____ de _____ .

h. They're her stockings. Son _____ medias.

i. They're HER stockings. Son _____ medias _____ .

j. They're hers. Son _____ .

Noun + *de* + noun/pronoun

This structure was introduced in Level One. You will remember that it literally means that an item is *of* another person.

| **el sombrero *de* Ricardo** | **the hat** *of Ricardo* |

We would normally translate that as *Ricardo's hat*, because that sounds most natural to English speakers. This structure can be used with prepositional pronouns also.

| **el sombrero *de* él** | **the hat** *of him (his hat)* |

Here are the prepositional pronouns for your reference:

mí (me)	**nosotros** / **nosotras** (us)
ti (you)	**vosotros** / **vosotras** (you)
él (him) **ella** (her) **Ud.** (you)	**ellos** (them) **ellas** (them) **Uds.** (you)

The prepositional pronouns are easy to memorize, because they are the same forms as the subject pronouns except for **mí** and **ti**.

Answer the questions.

2.6
a. Which two prepositional pronouns are different? _____

b. What are some examples of Spanish prepositions? _____

It is most important to remember the apostrophe + s ('s) is used only in English. Do not use it in Spanish to show possession.

Replace the proper nouns in each expression with a prepositional pronoun. Rewrite each sentence in Spanish.

2.7
a. Son los zapatos de la abuela. _____

b. Es la chaqueta de Jorge. _____

c. Es el vestido largo de la princesa. _____

d. Son las botas de la Sra. Muñoz. _____

e. Es el collar de ti y de mí. _____

f. Es la cadena de oro de mi padre. _____

g. Es la ropa de Julio y Beto. _____

h. Es el traje de baño de su amiga. _____

Review using **noun + *de* + noun/pronoun** by completing the translations below.

Do this exercise with your instructor. Translate the following sentences. Notice the absence of the apostrophe + s ('s) in Spanish.

2.8
a. Es el abrigo de Raúl. _____

b. Es el paraguas de MariCarmen. _____

c. Son los pantalones de mi papá. _____

d. Es la falda de la señora. _____

e. Trae la camiseta de Ud. _____

f. Se pone las chaquetas de Jorge y de Guillermo. _____

g. Yo tengo las joyas de nosotros. _____

h. He is wearing my boots. _____

i. Is it Elena's dress? _____

j. You have his sweater. _____

k. You put on Pedro's cap. _____

l. She is wearing Cristina's skirt. _____

m. I try on your sneakers. _____

n. Does he have his jacket? _____

o. Where is my new blouse? _____

✓ Adult check _____
                                             Initial   Date

Possessive Adjectives

A shorter way to express possession is with possessive adjectives. This topic, too, was introduced in Level One, so we will have only a short review here.

Some examples of possessive adjectives in English include: **my**, **your**, **his**, **our**, and **their**.

Read the following Spanish phrases.

Mis zapatos son negros.	*My* shoes are black.
Nuestras joyas son caras.	*Our* jewelry is expensive.
Tus guantes son apretados.	*Your* gloves are tight.

Answer the following questions.

2.9 a. Where is the possessive adjective placed (in relation to the noun it's describing)? _____
_____

b. When a possessive adjective is used, do you also need a definite (or indefinite) article? _____

c. In the first example, why is *mis* used, if *mi*s refers to only one person? _____
_____

d. In the second example, we know that *nuestras* is not necessarily a group of females.
Why is the feminine plural used here? _____

e. Does *tus* mean there is more than one of *you* in the last example? _____
_____

This is an important point: Possessive adjectives agree in **meaning** with the owner but in **number** and **gender** with the item(s) owned.

Let's review the possessive adjectives. Complete the chart by filling in the English possessive adjectives equivalent to the Spanish prepositional phrases given.

2.10

mi (de mí)	a. _____	nuestro(a)(s) (de nosotros/as)	f. _____
ti (de ti)	b. _____	vuestro(a)(s) (de vosotros/as)	g. _____
su(s) (de él) (de ella) (de Ud.)	c. _____ d. _____ e. _____	su(s) (de ellos) (de ellas) (de Uds.)	h. _____ i. _____

Fill in the blank with the appropriate agreeing possessive adjective.

2.11
a. ¿Buscas _____ joyas? (my)
b. Tienes _____ ropa. (her)
c. ¿Te gusta comprar _____ ropa en el centro comercial? (his)
d. ¿Dónde está _____ mochila. (our)
e. _____ calcetines son blancos. (Their)
f. Las llaves están en _____ bolsa. (your, friendly)
g. _____ hermanos necesitan ponerse zapatos nuevos para ir a la boda. (Your, friendly)
h. ¿Devolvió _____ madre estos pantalones? (our)
i. Un ladrón robó _____ billetera. (my)
j. _____ ropa es muy fina. (Their)

Choose and circle the agreeing possessive adjective.

2.12
a. (Su/Sus) chaqueta está en la mochila.
b. (Su/Sus) vestido es muy elegante.
c. No sabe donde están (mi/mis) zapatos.
d. (Nuestros/Nuestras) pendientes son de oro.
e. (Su/Sus) gorra* se pierde a causa del viento.

*Note: Contrary to English, the article of clothing is in the singular here, even though the subject is plural, because each person has only one cap.

f. Mi madre compró (tu/tus) suéter ayer.

g. El traje es para (nuestro/nuestros) padre.

h. (Mi/Mis) mochila está llena.

i. ¿Por qué no lavas (nuestras/nuestros) cortinas?

j. Es necesario llevar (su/sus) zapatos de tacones bajos.

Restate the possessive expressions with a possessive adjective. That is, replace the noun + *de* + noun/pronoun expression with a possessive adjective.

Example: Es el libro de mí.
            Es mi libro.

2.13   a.   Es el collar de ella. _____

b.   Es la bolsa de nosotros. _____

c.   Es el paraguas de Uds. _____

d.   Son los zapatos de María. _____

e.   Es el suéter de nosotros. _____

f.   Necesito usar las camisas de Paco. _____

g.   ¿Dónde están las medias de mí? _____

h.   Prefieren el traje de baño de Ud. _____

i.   Quieren ver el vestido nuevo de ti. _____

j.   Llevo la ropa de ellos al sastre. _____

Translate the italicized adjectives in order to complete the Spanish sentences.

2.14   a.   ¿Te pones (*his*) chaqueta? _____

b.   Se olvidó de traer (*my*) boots. _____

c.   Cuelga (*her*) suéter. _____

d.   Lavan (*your/friendly*) ropa. _____

e.   Consuelo plancha (*our*) camisas. _____

f.   Le prestó a ella (*my*) blusa. _____

g.   Encontraron (*her*) aretes en la bolsa. _____

h.   ¿Dónde están (*their*) paraguas? _____

i.   Él está llevando (*your/formal*) traje elegante. _____

j.   Ella necesita (*your/friendly*) medias. _____

Answer the questions in complete Spanish sentences. Pay close attention to the change of adjectives from question to answer.

2.15 a. ¿Dónde están tus libros? _____

b. ¿Perdiste sus llaves? _____

c. ¿Dónde puso Papá mi mochila? _____

d. ¿Viste mi pulsera? _____

e. ¿Quién tiene su bolsa? _____

f. ¿Lavas la ropa de tu hermano? _____
_____

g. ¿Te pones las camisetas de tus amigos? _____
_____

h. ¿Quiere Enrique llevar tu corbata nueva? _____

i. ¿Dónde están tus tarjetas de crédito? _____
_____

j. ¿A veces usas el lápiz del profesor? _____

✔ Adult check _____
  Initial   Date

Stressed Possessive Adjectives

Examine the following two Spanish sentences:

Necesito mi mochila.

Necesito la mochila mía.

They both communicate *I need my backpack.* The difference is that the **second** sentence carries extra emphasis on the idea of **my**. Think of it this way:

I need MY backpack.

In the Spanish language, unlike English, the tone of voice is not used to stress certain words and ideas in sentences. This is one reason the Spanish language sounds so "fast" to non-speakers. Instead, different words and structures add emphasis and stress to ideas. This is where the **stressed possessive adjectives** come in.

Compare the following expressions:

Mi corbata es fina.	My tie is fine.
La corbata mía es fina.	MY tie is fine.
Nuestra ropa es cara.	Our clothing is expensive.
La ropa nuestra es cara.	OUR clothing is more expensive.

Fill in the translations on your own this time.

2.16 a. Mi falda es larga. *My skirt is long.* _____

La falda suya es más larga. _____

b. ¿Es tu vestido verde? *Is your dress green?* _____

No, el vestido mío es azul. _____

c. Nuestras joyas son bonitas. *Our jewelry is pretty.* _____

Las joyas suyas son más bonitas. _____

Compare the two kinds of possessive adjectives. Answer the questions.

2.17 a. Is the stressed possessive adjective placed before or after its noun? _____

b. With what does it agree in number and gender? _____

c. Is the definite article a part of this expression? _____

d. What is the function of the stressed possessive adjective? _____
_____

e. Which of the stressed possessive adjectives are the same as the non-stressed? _____
_____

Write the stressed possessive adjectives in the appropriate location in the chart.

2.18

el/los a. _____		el/los g. _____	
la/las b. _____		la/las h. _____	
(MY)		(OUR)	
el/los c. _____		el/los vuestro(s)	
la/las d. _____		la/las vuestra(s)	
(YOUR)		(YOUR)	
el/los e. _____		el/los i. _____	
la/las f. _____		la/las j. _____	
(HIS, HER, YOUR)		(THEIR, YOUR)	

Choose and circle the correct agreeing adjective.

2.19 a. HIS shirt is ugly.

(El, La) camisa (suyo, suya) es fea.

b. That is YOUR skirt.

Ésa es (el, la) falda (mía, tuya).

c. I don't need MY jacket.

No necesito (el, la) chaqueta (mía, mío).

d. OUR shoes are in the closet.

(Los, Las) zapatos (nuestros, nuestro) están en el armario.

e. I don't want to look for HER purse.

No quiero buscar (la, las) bolsa (suya, tuya).

f. Well, YOUR dress is very casual.

Pues, (los, el) vestido (suya, suyo) es muy informal.

g. MY socks are yellow too.

(Los, Las) calcetines (míos, mías) son amarillos también.

h. This is not HIS bathing suit.

Éste no es (la, el) traje de baño (nuestro, suyo).

i. I didn't give MY umbrella to you.

No te di (el, los) paraguas (mío, míos).

j. YOUR tie is more expensive than my tie.

(El, La) corbata (suya, suyas) es más cara que mi corbata.

 Complete the translations by filling in the missing terms.

2.20 a. I don't like HER gold chain.

No me gusta _____ cadena de oro _____ .

b. HIS boots are older than MY boots.

_____ botas _____ son más viejas que mis botas.

c. We prefer OUR blue T-shirts.

Preferimos _____ camisetas azules _____ .

d. You buy YOUR clothing at the mall. (your, friendly)

Compras _____ ropa _____ en el centro comercial.

SPANISH II LIFEPAC FOUR TEST

Name _____

Date _____

Score _____

119 / 149

LISTENING

1. Paco is describing what clothing he sees on other people. Listen to each description carefully. For each question, circle the items you heard mentioned. Also, make note of the qualities he describes. [CD–C, Track 10] (1 pt. each)

    1. a. a scarf   b. a hat   c. a tie   d. _____
    2. a. pants   b. a skirt   c. a suit   d. _____
    3. a. a jacket   b. a coat   c. a sweater   d. _____
    4. a. a bracelet   b. a necklace   c. earrings   d. _____
    5. a. a suit   b. a bathing suit   c. jeans   d. _____
    6. a. socks   b. stockings   c. gloves   d. _____
    7. a. a shirt   b. a T-shirt   c. a blouse   d. _____
    8. a. a bag/purse   b. a wallet   c. a blouse   d. _____
    9. a. an umbrella   b. high-heeled shoes c. a necklace   d. _____
    10. a. boots   b. pajamas   c. a tie   d. _____

2. Whose supplies are these? For each sentence you hear, make a note of who owns them by circling the agreeing English expression. [CD–C, Track 11] (1 pt. each)

    1. a. my   b. his   c. your
    2. a. our   b. my   c. her
    3. a. his   b. our   c. her
    4. a. your   b. their   c. his
    5. a. their   b. your   c. my
    6. a. our   b. her   c. my
    7. a. my   b. your (formal)   c. your (friendly)
    8. a. our   b. her   c. my
    9. a. my   b. his   c. their
    10. a. all of your b. his   c. your (friendly)

3. **Label each picture with the letter of the correct sentence as you hear each description.**
   [CD–C, Track 12] (1 pt. each)

1. _____ 2. _____ 3. _____ 4. _____ 5. _____

6. _____ 7. _____ 8. _____ 9. _____ 10. _____

WRITING

4. **Choose and circle the correct identifying term for the items pictured.** (1 pt. each)

a. una gorra /
   una bufanda

b. los calcetines /
   las medias

c. la camisa /
   la blusa

d. la camisa /
   la camiseta

e. el vestido /
   la falda

f. los pendientes /
   los aretes

g. un cinturón /
   una bolsa

h. una gorra /
   un sombrero

i. unos pantalones /
   un short

j. una cadena de
   oro / una cadena
   de plata

5. **Complete the statements by filling in the opposite of each italicized quality.** (1 pt. each)

   a. El vestido no es *nuevo*, sino _____ .

   b. La falda no es *informal*, sino _____ .

   c. La cadena de plata no es *corta*, sino _____ .

   d. La camiseta no es azul *oscuro*, sino azul _____ .

   e. El sombrero no está *limpio*, sino _____ .

   f. Mis zapatos no son de tacones *altos*, sino zapatos de tacones _____ .

   g. Esta blusa no es *bonita*, sino _____ .

   h. Los vaqueros no son *caros*, sino _____ .

   i. La mochila no es *grande*, sino _____ .

   j. La corbata no es *ancha*, sino _____ .

6. **Answer the questions about the pictures, using complete Spanish sentences. Do not repeat any adjectives in this activity.** (2 pts. each)

a. ¿Qué tipo de camisa tienes?

_____
_____

b. ¿Qué tipo de corbata llevas?

_____
_____

c. ¿Qué tipo de vestido te pones?

_____
_____

d. ¿Qué tipo de pantalones lleva Ud.?

_____
_____

 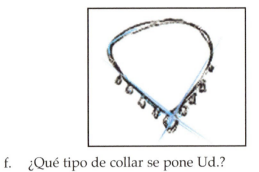

e. ¿Qué tipo de falda compras?　　　　　　f. ¿Qué tipo de collar se pone Ud.?

_____　　　　_____

_____　　　　_____

7. **Decide what articles of clothing or personal accessories are being described. Write the appropriate Spanish term with its definite article.** (1 pt. each)

    a. la "ropa" que lleva a la cama　　_____

    b. la ropa que cubre las manos　　_____

    c. la ropa formal para caballeros　　_____

    d. los zapatos para los deportes　　_____

    e. unos pantalones muy informales　　_____

    f. la ropa para nadar　　_____

    g. una joya para los dedos　　_____

    h. la ropa que cubre la cabeza　　_____

    i. donde se pone el dinero　　_____

    j. donde un estudiante lleva los libros　　_____

8. **Translate the following into English.** (2 pts. each)

    a. Los niños se ponen los tenis nuevos.

    _____

    b. Para mi cumpleaños, mi abuela me compra la ropa interior.

    _____

    c. ¿Esta blusa es bastante apretada, no?

    _____

    d. Obtengo las medias de color café claro.

    _____

    e. Los pendientes de oro son muy caros.

    _____

Translate the following into Spanish. (2 pts. each)

f. He buys fine shoes.

g. She puts on a cheap scarf.

h. I'm going to bring the old umbrella.

i. You (Ud.) have a pretty skirt.

j. They wear casual pants.

9. **Respond to each question affirmatively and concisely, thus replacing the longer expression of possession with a possessive pronoun.** (1 pt. each)

   Example: ¿Es la casa de Elena?
   Sí, es suya.

   a. ¿Es la hermana de Pablo?

   b. ¿Trajiste el cuaderno de ti?

   c. ¿Necesitas la ayuda de nosotros?

   d. ¿Tienes la bolsa de mí?

   e. ¿Escribiste las cartas de Alonso?

   f. ¿Tiene ella el juguete de Uds.?

10. **Change the stressed possessive adjectives to the unstressed possessive adjectives.** (1 pt. each)

    Example: Aquí está la casa mía.
    Aquí está mi casa.

    a. Obtienen el dinero suyo en el banco.

    b. No puedo ver la prima nuestra.

c. Consiguen las frutas suyas del mercado.
_____

d. Traigo el traje mío.
_____

e. Pierden los guantes suyos.
_____

f. Los papeles tuyos están sobre la mesa.
_____

11. **Express possession in FOUR different ways for each statement given.** (1 pt. each blank)

   a. my jacket _____   _____

   _____   _____

   b. Pablo's shirts _____   _____

   _____   _____

   c. our car _____   _____

   _____   _____

   d. your *(tú)* suits _____   _____

   _____   _____

12. **Write the present participle for each infinitive given.** (1 pt. each)

   a. jugar _____   h. querer _____
   b. escribir _____   i. sentirse _____
   c. traer _____   j. decir _____
   d. venir _____   k. creer _____
   e. encontrar _____ l. pedir _____
   f. ir _____   m. perder _____
   g. dormir _____   n. leer _____

13. **Complete the sentences with the infinitive or the present participle.** (1 pt. each)

   a. Al _____ ella nos dijo la verdad. (llegar)

   b. _____ con mis amigos es muy divertido. (ir de compras)

   c. Sí, sí, Mamá, me estoy _____ la chaqueta. (quitar)

   d. ¿_____ el español es difícil? ¡No, es fácil! (aprender)

   e. Me salté a los pies, _____ el nombre del campeón. (gritar)

   f. Ud. tropieza, _____ a la tierra. (caerse)

   g. Leí el libro, _____ una pista (clue) al misterio. (buscar)

   h. A ti te gusta _____ al ajedrez. (jugar)

   i. Estoy cansada de _____ esta canción. (oír)

   j. Perdóneme, Ud. está _____ muy rápidamente. (hablar)

READING

Read the following passage and answer the comprehension questions that follow.

Ayuda para seleccionar un regalo

Comprar la ropa para otras personas, como regalo, puede ser difícil. Uno necesita saber mucho: ¿De qué talla es la persona? ¿Cuáles colores prefiere (los claros o los oscuros)? Generalmente, ¿cómo se viste? ¿Prefiere la ropa elegante o informal? ¿Qué necesita —la ropa formal para el trabajo o algo más informal o deportivo? Y por fin, no se olvide de que la ropa puede ser cara. A veces comprar más de una camisa puede ser difícil cuando no hay mucho que gastar.

Tenemos unas sugerencias:

Todo el mundo siempre puede usar la ropa interior o los calcetines. Siempre son regalos útiles. No tienen que costar muchísimo tampoco. Se venden en una variedad de colores y son fáciles de encontrar en muchas tiendas.

Si la ropa interior es un regalo demasiado personal, se puede comprar un sombrero o una gorra. Quizás una corbata para los caballeros o una bufanda fina para las damas. De esta manera, no tiene que preocuparse de la talla. Los precios de estos complementos son variados, como los estilos y los colores.

Nuestra sugerencia final es de dar dinero o un certificado de regalo para una tienda favorita. Algunos creen que el dinero no es buen regalo. Entonces, puede llevar al otro de compras. La persona puede escoger el regalo perfecto.

Bueno. ¿Son algunas de estas ideas nuevas para Ud.? Espero que sí. ¡Buena suerte!

14. **Multiple choice: Choose and circle the best response to each question based on the reading.**
    (1 pt. each)

    1. The main goal of this article is. . .
        a. to offer help in choosing gifts.
        b. to suggest the best place to buy clothing.
        c. to offer advice on how to return a gift.

    2. According to the article, why can buying clothes as a gift be problematic?
        a. The recipient may not like it.
        b. The stores are too far away.
        c. There are many unknowns to consider.

    3. One article of clothing suggested is. . .
        a. a hat.
        b. jewelry.
        c. elegant clothing.

    4. According to the article, why do socks make a good gift?
        a. They go with anything.
        b. They are very expensive.
        c. Everyone needs socks.

    5. What does the article suggest as a final option?
        a. Buy a scarf.
        b. Buy a tie.
        c. Take the person shopping with you.

e. Did you know that HIS shoes are from Italy?

¿Sabías que _____ zapatos _____ son de Italia?

f. MY belt is leather.

_____ cinturón _____ es de cuero.

g. ¿Where are YOUR sneakers? (your, formal)

¿Dónde están _____ tenis _____?

h. We buy OUR bracelets at that store.

Compramos _____ pulseras _____ en esa tienda.

i. Are those MY blouses?

¿Son ésas _____ blusas _____?

j. OUR hats are cleaner than his.

_____ sombreros _____ están más limpios que los suyos.

Rewrite these possessive expressions, using the stressed possessive adjectives.

2.21 a. Yo tengo las llaves de Ud.

_____

b. ¿Por qué quieren la billetera de ti?

_____

c. Ellos trajeron la chaqueta de mí.

_____

d. Ellas buscan las joyas de Uds.

_____

e. Me pongo la falda de Mamá.

_____

f. Vendieron la ropa de nosotros.

_____

g. El señor Pacheco es un amigo de mí.

_____

h. No entiendo por qué llevas los zapatos de él.

_____

i. Él ladrón roba las joyas de nosotros.
_____

j. Él devuelve el paraguas de Ud.
_____

Express the following phrases, using each of the three ways we have reviewed.

2.22 1. my shorts
    a. _____
    b. _____
    c. _____

2. his gold chain
    a. _____
    b. _____
    c. _____

3. our clothing
    a. _____
    b. _____
    c. _____

4. her stockings
    a. _____
    b. _____
    c. _____

5. his belt
    a. _____
    b. _____
    c. _____

6. our bedroom
    a. _____
    b. _____
    c. _____

7. your (formal) sister
    a. _____
    b. _____
    c. _____

8. your (friendly) garage
    a. _____
    b. _____
    c. _____

9. my backpack
    a. _____
    b. _____
    c. _____

10. your (all of you) T-shirts
    a. _____
    b. _____
    c. _____

Answer the questions in complete Spanish sentences, using the appropriate stressed possessive adjective in each answer.

2.23 a. ¿De qué color es la casa tuya?
_____

b. ¿Quién es el mejor amigo tuyo?
_____

c. ¿Es grande el coche de tu padre?

d. ¿Puedes hacer la tarea mía?

e. ¿Cuándo viene su madre (de Uds.) para recogerlos?

f. ¿Es el cuaderno tuyo azul o amarillo?

g. ¿Cómo describes tu familia?

h. ¿Cómo es tu mejor amiga?

i. ¿Es tu cumpleaños el nueve de abril?

j. ¿Está sucio el dormitorio de tu hermano(a)?

✔ Adult check _____
Initial   Date

Possessive Pronouns

The final method of expressing the possessive is the possessive pronoun. The possessive pronoun has three functions in a Spanish sentence:

- ✔ It replaces (and references) the item owned.
- ✔ It agrees with that item in number and gender.
- ✔ It expresses someone's ownership.

The English term "pronoun" can be deceiving, for it suggests a single word. Remember to pair the possessive term with a definite article—thus, two words are needed—to form the possessive pronoun.

 Answer the questions.

2.24 a. How does a pronoun work within a sentence? _____

b. How is the possessive pronoun formed in Spanish? _____

The possessive pronouns are the same forms as the stressed possessive adjectives, except they are preceded by the definite article or some other determiner, except after the verb *ser*. Instead of modifying a noun, they replace it.

Rewrite each sentence using a possessive pronoun. Do not rewrite the item owned.
Remember, the pronoun will agree in number and gender with the noun it replaces.

Example: Es el coche de él.   **Es suyo.**

2.25
a. Es el traje suyo.   _____
b. Son los zapatos de Ud.   _____
c. Son los libros de José.   _____
d. Es mi casa.   _____
e. Son nuestros pantalones.   _____
f. Son los amigos tuyos.   _____
g. Es la casa de ella.   _____
h. Son sus vestidos.   _____
i. Son las mochilas de Uds.   _____

Complete the chart by filling in the singular and the plural possessive pronouns. Include the definite articles.

2.26

(mine)	(ours)
a. _____	m. _____
b. _____	n. _____
c. _____	o. _____
d. _____	p. _____
(yours)	**(yours)**
e. _____	el vuestro
f. _____	la vuestra
g. _____	los vuestros
h. _____	las vuestras
(his, hers, yours)	**(theirs, yours)**
i. _____	q. _____
j. _____	r. _____
k. _____	s. _____
l. _____	t. _____

Let's analyze some of these in sentences. Read the following sample question and answer.

¿De qué color es el libro de MariCarmen?	What color is MariCarmen's book?
El suyo es rojo.	Hers is red.

Answer the questions about the sample above.

2.27 a. Does a male or female own the book? _____

b. Which possessive pronoun is used? _____

c. Is that pronoun masculine or feminine? _____

d. Does this mean MariCarmen has to be a boy? _____

e. How can a masculine pronoun refer to a girl? _____

_____

Read this sample sentence.

Las chaquetas azules son nuestras.	The blue jackets are ours.

Answer the questions about the sample above.

2.28 a. Do we know for sure whether the jackets are owned by men or women? _____

b. Does *nuestras* give us that kind of information? _____

c. Why, then, is *nuestras* feminine and plural? _____

_____

Pay close attention to the agreement with what is owned as you begin, and eventually the expression of agreement will come naturally to you.

Rewrite each sentence, replacing the expression of possession with an agreeing possessive pronoun.

Group 1 (noun + **de** + noun/pronoun)

2.29 a. Usas la computadora de él. _____

b. Tienen los tenis de Uds. _____

c. Limpiamos el dormitorio de nosotras. _____

d. Necesito los libros de mí. _____

e. La abuelita trajo las galletas favoritas de ti. _____

Rewrite each sentence, replacing the expression of possession with an agreeing possessive pronoun.

Group 2 (possessive adjectives)

2.30 a. No puedo ver mi coche.

      b. Diste de comer a sus conejos.

      c. Compra tus libros.

      d. Sacamos nuestras fotos.

      e. ¿Dónde compra Ud. sus joyas normalmente?

Rewrite each sentence, replacing the expression of possession with an agreeing possessive pronoun.

Group 3 (stressed possessive adjectives)

2.31 a. ¿No te gusta la amiga suya?

      b. Prefiero la música nuestra.

      c. Escribe con el bolígrafo suyo.

      d. ¿Bebieron todos los refrescos tuyos?

      e. ¿Dónde están los aretes míos?

You're sure that you remembered to bring everything you needed to a picnic with friends at the beach. Many others forgot some things. Complete the expressions by using a possessive pronoun. Follow the example.

Example: Yo traje una manta, pero Carmen no *trajo la suya.*

2.32
a. Tengo una bebida, pero tú _____.

b. No me olvidé de traer la loción bronceadora, pero Eduardo _____.

c. Tengo algunos sandwiches deliciosos, pero Elena y Luis _____.

d. Llevo las gafas de sol, pero Uds. _____.

e. Llevo mi mochila también, pero Chamo y tú _____.

f. ¡Ay de mí! Luis tiene el traje de baño, pero yo _____.

g. Afortunadamente yo traigo las llaves para el coche, pero mis amigos _____.

h. ¡Ay de mí! Esas personas tienen un estéreo, pero nosotros _____.

i. Tengo el dinero conmigo, pero Ud. _____.

j. Traigo un tenedor, una cuchara y un cuchillo, pero Jorge _____.

Optional Activities. See the Answer Key.

As you and your family prepare to leave for vacation, your mother is double-checking everyone's suitcases, making sure all is packed. Answer her questions affirmatively or negatively, according to the cues. Use the possessive pronouns in your responses. Follow the example.

Example: ¿Tienes la ropa interior de ti? (sí)
Sí, tengo la mía.

2.33
a. ¿Tiene Papá la aspirina? (no)

_____

b. ¿Tenemos los billetes de nosotros? (sí)

_____

c. ¿Tiene Consuelo la chaqueta? (sí)

_____

d. ¿Tengo yo los zapatos bajos? (no)

_____

e. ¿Tienes el dinero de ti? (sí)

_____

f. ¿Tienen sus hermanos los discos compactos de ellos? (no)

_____

g. ¿Tienes la bolsa de ti? (sí)
_____

h. ¿Tienen Consuelo y Cristóbal las almohadas? (sí)
_____

i. ¿Tiene Papá los anteojos? (no)
_____

j. ¿Tengo yo la medicina? (sí)
_____

¡Felicidades! You have learned four different ways to express possession in Spanish.

Describe what each person owns in these four ways: a) noun + *de* + noun/pronoun, b) the possessive adjective, c) the stressed possessive adjective, and d) the possessive pronoun. Follow the example.

Example: una billetera fina/el presidente de la compañía

    a. **Es la billetera fina del presidente de la compañía.** c. **Es la billetera suya.**

    b. **Es su billetera.**   d. **Es suya.**

2.34 1. la cadena/la señora

    a. _____   c. _____

    b. _____   d. _____

  2. la gorra/mi amigo

    a. _____   c. _____

    b. _____   d. _____

  3. el coche/nosotros

    a. _____   c. _____

    b. _____   d. _____

  4. los zapatos/yo

    a. _____   c. _____

    b. _____   d. _____

  5. los anteojos/tú

    a. _____   c. _____

    b. _____   d. _____

Change the possessive expressions as needed to agree with each new subject.

2.35 1. mi familia

   a. our family _____

   b. his family _____

   c. your (formal) family _____

2. las suyas

   a. his _____

   b. ours _____

   c. mine _____

3. el dormitorio nuestro

   a. Pedro's room _____

   b. MY room _____

   c. YOUR (formal) room _____

4. mis primas

   a. HIS cousins _____

   b. Verónica's cousins _____

   c. ours _____

5. tu computadora

   a. YOUR (friendly) computer _____

   b. your (formal) computer _____

   c. mine _____

Choose and circle the correct choices to complete each sentence.

2.36 a. I need to use your pen.

   Necesito usar (el, la) bolígrafo (nuestro, suyo, mío).

b. His suit is wrinkled.

   (Un, El) traje (su, suyo, nuestro) está arrugado.

c. Where are my keys? Where are yours?

   ¿Dónde están (las, la) llaves (mías, mis, suyas)? ¿Dónde están (la, las) (ti, tus, tuyas)?

d. Your brother is taller than mine.

   (De Ud., Suyo, Su) hermano es más alto que (el, un) (mía, mío, mí).

e. We have our homework here.

Nosotros tenemos (nuestro, de nosotros, nuestra) tarea aquí.

f. Can I read your newspaper? I lost mine.

¿Puedo leer (su, de él, sus) periódico? Perdí (el mío, los míos, mis).

g. Their articles? Well, his is good, but I don't like her article.

¿Los artículos (de Ud., de Uds., de ellos)? Pues, (de él, el suyo, su) es bueno, pero no me gusta el artículo (de ella, de Ud., su).

h. My father has to drive my brother home.

El padre (de mí, mi, mis) tiene que llevar al hermano (mía, míos, mío) a casa en carro.

i. Enrique's girlfriend is very nice.

(El, La, Los) novia (de Enrique, su, suyo) es muy simpática.

j. Hey! The house is big! That's his!

¡Oye! La casa es grande. ¡Ésa es (mío, suya, mía)!

Beto's family has just moved. They are unpacking some of their things. Read their conversation out loud with two partners, or one person can play two roles. (Elisa is Beto's sister.)

2.37

Beto: ¿Dónde están mis cosas? Quiero ponerlas en el dormitorio de mí.

Elisa: Esta caja (box) es mía. Beto, busca la tuya allí.

Beto: ¡Ésta debe ser la caja mía!

Mamá: Lo siento, Beto. Las cosas en esta caja son las cosas de nuestro padre.

Elisa: Puedo ayudarte. ¿Qué necesitas?

Beto: Quiero encontrar la caja de mi ropa. Necesito calcetines limpios.

Elisa: ¡Ajá! Mira, Beto, yo encontré los tuyos!

Beto: Gracias, Elisa.

✓ Adult check _____
Initial   Date

LISTENING EXERCISES II

Exercise 1. Who could be the owner of each item? Based on what you hear, circle your answer. [CD–C, Track 4]

	Example: Es la casa de Ud.	he is	she is	(you are)
a.	they are	I am		we are
b.	she is	we are		you are
c.	I am	you are		we are
d.	we are	I am		he is
e.	you are	all of you are		they are
f.	she is	we are		I am
g.	they are	you are		she is
h.	we are	they are		all of you are
i.	I am	he is		you are
j.	they are	we are		you are

Exercise 2. Again, who could be the owner of each item? This time, choose the appropriate possessive adjective. [CD–C, Track 5]

	Example: la casa suya	tu	sus	(su)
a.	tu	su		mi
b.	mis	sus		nuestra
c.	tu	su		nuestro
d.	sus	tus		mis
e.	mi	su		nuestro
f.	tu	su		mi
g.	su	nuestra		sus
h.	mi	nuestro		tu
i.	tu	nuestra		su
j.	mis	sus		tu

Exercise 3. Choose and circle the agreeing possessive pronoun, based upon each statement you hear. [CD–C, Track 6]

	Example: Su casa es grande.	el tuyo	(la suya)	el suyo
a.	el mío	la mía	la nuestra	
b.	el nuestro	la nuestra	los nuestros	
c.	el suyo	las suyas	la suya	
d.	los tuyos	el tuyo	la tuya	
e.	la suya	la nuestra	las suyas	
f.	las suyas	las tuyas	los tuyos	
g.	el nuestro	la nuestra	la suya	
h.	el mío	las mías	las suyas	
i.	los tuyos	los nuestros	las tuyas	
j.	la mía	la suya	los suyos	

Adult check
                Initial   Date

 Review the material in this section in preparation for the Self Test. This Self Test will check your mastery of this particular section as well as your knowledge of the previous section.

SELF TEST 2

2.01 Answer the questions in complete Spanish sentences. Use the cues provided and the noun + *de* + noun/pronoun method of expression. (2 pts. each)

Example: ¿De quién es la computadora? (nosotras)
Es la computadora de nosotras.

a. ¿De quiénes son los vestidos? (las señoras)

b. ¿De quiénes son las galletas? (los niños)

c. ¿De quién es el anillo? (Ud.)

d. ¿De quién son los mapas? (la clase)

e. ¿De quién es la tarea? (la profesora de inglés)

f. ¿De quién es la tarjeta? (tú)

g. ¿De quiénes son los pendientes? (Uds.)

h. ¿De quién es el periódico? (yo)

i. ¿De quién es la foto? (Elena)

j. ¿De quién es la bicicleta? (él)

2.02 Rewrite the sentences with unstressed possessive adjectives. (2 pts. each)

a. Prefiero visitar al primo de Ud.

b. No puedes usar el coche de nosotros.

c. Nosotros perdimos el anillo de Mamá.

d. Escucha el disco de Uds.

e. Escribí una carta al amigo de mí.

f. ¿Por qué estás llevando las botas de Víctor?

g. Los chicos caminaron por el césped de la mujer vieja.

h. ¿Estás mirando el examen de sus vecinos?

i. ¿Son los hermanos de ti?

j. Aprendiste mucho de la familia de nosotros.

2.03 **Rewrite the sentences, using the appropriate stressed possessive adjective in each response.** (2 pts. each.)

a. Son los zapatos de Ud.

b. Es tú calculadora.

c. Son mis calcetines.

d. Es la camisa de Pablo.

e. Son las cadenas de Elena.

f. Es la revista de nosotros.

2.04 **Respond to each question positively. Use a possessive pronoun in your answer. Follow the example.** (2 pts. each)

Example: ¿Tienes tus papeles?
Sí, tengo los míos.

a. ¿Leíste sus revistas?
_____

b. ¿Viste nuestro artículo en el periódico?
_____

c. ¿Escribiste su anuncio (de ellas)?
_____

d. ¿Llamaste a tu abuelita?
_____

e. ¿Habló Ud. con mis tíos?
_____

f. ¿Comprendieron ellos su anuncio (de Ud.)?
_____

g. ¿Prefirieron Uds. nuestra sopa?
_____

h. ¿Vieron ellos a mi novia?
_____

i. ¿Perdieron ellos mis cuadernos?
_____

j. ¿Encontraron ellas los lápices (de él)?
_____

58 / 72

Score _____
Adult check _____
           Initial   Date

III. GRAMMAR: THE PRESENT PARTICIPLE

The present participle is used in adverbial phrases as well as in the progressive tenses.

The present participial ending for -ar verbs is -ando.

The present participial ending for -er/-ir verbs is -iendo.

The English equivalent of these endings is -ing.

Therefore, if *llevar* means "to wear," then the English translation for *llevando* is "wearing."

Write the present participle of each of these regular infinitives in the first column. Then write its English translation in the second column.

		Present participle	Translation
3.1	1. buscar	a. _____	b. _____
	2. vivir	a. _____	b. _____
	3. tener	a. _____	b. _____
	4. estudiar	a. _____	b. _____
	5. asistir	a. _____	b. _____
	6. cantar	a. _____	b. _____
	7. abrir	a. _____	b. _____
	8. pensar	a. _____	b. _____
	9. poner	a. _____	b. _____
	10. subir	a. _____	b. _____

Infinitives that end in *-eer*, *-aer*, and *-uir* have a spelling change in the present participle.

The *i* (of *-iendo*) changes to *y*. For example, *leer* becomes *leyendo*.

The same rule applies to the verb *ir*, which has no other letters before the participial ending: *yendo*.

Write the present participle of each infinitive in the first column. Then, write its English translation in the second column.

          Present participle   **Translation**

3.2
1. creer   a. _____   b. _____
2. traer   a. _____   b. _____
3. poseer   a. _____   b. _____
4. huir   a. _____   b. _____
5. influir   a. _____   b. _____
6. caer   a. _____   b. _____
7. leer   a. _____   b. _____
8. construir   a. _____   b. _____
9. oír   a. _____   b. _____
10. ir   a. _____   b. _____

The *-ir* stem-changing (shoe) verbs also have spelling changes in the present participle.

The *o* in verbs like *dormir* changes to *u*. For example, *dormir* becomes *durmiendo*.

The *e* in verbs like *sentir* changes to *i*. For example, *sentir* becomes *sintiendo*.

Write the present participle and its English translation for each verb given.

          Present participle   **Translation**

3.3
1. divertir   a. _____   b. _____
2. preferir   a. _____   b. _____
3. vestir   a. _____   b. _____
4. pedir   a. _____   b. _____
5. impedir   a. _____   b. _____
6. morir   a. _____   b. _____
7. servir   a. _____   b. _____
8. seguir   a. _____   b. _____
9. dormir   a. _____   b. _____

Finally, there are a few irregular present participles to learn:

decir   *diciendo*
poder   *pudiendo*
venir   *viniendo*

Note also that *ser* becomes *siendo* and *ver* becomes *viendo*.

Now we'll examine how the Spanish present participle form can be used in other constructions.

Read the following sentences. Write the English equivalent below each.

3.4   a.   La niña sigue llorando a sus padres.

   _____

   b.   El profesor continúa hablando mientras suena el teléfono.

   _____

   c.   Yo vengo corriendo para saludar a Uds.

   _____

The present participles *llorando*, *hablando*, and *corriendo* have descriptive functions in each sentence.

Answer the questions.

3.5   a.   What does *llorando* describe? _____

   b.   What does *hablando* describe? _____

   c.   What does *corriendo* describe? _____

   d.   In each case, what part of speech does the present participle describe? _____

   e.   The present participle describes HOW a VERB (or action) is performed. Thus, what part of speech does the present participle function as?_____

Remember: **In Spanish, one of the functions of the present participle is to act as an adverb. In this case, it is linked to and describes the main action of a sentence. It is neither the main action nor the subject of the sentence, however.**

Study the following examples:

1. He leaves the room, shouting. (salir/gritar)
    Él sale gritando del cuarto.

2. We follow him, talking. (seguir/hablar)
    Nosotros lo seguimos hablando.

3. They left, kicking and screaming. (irse, dar patadas, gritar)
   Se fueron dando patadas y gritando.

4. You work, whistling a song. (trabajar, silbar)
   Trabajas silbando una canción.

5. I say good-bye, feeling sad. (despedirse, sentirse)
   Me despido sintiéndome triste.

6. I walk along the sidewalk, reading a book. (andar, leer)
   Ando por la acera, leyendo un libro.

7. She runs crying from the room. (correr, llorar)
   Élla corre llorando del cuarto.

8. You look at him, noting his dirty clothes. (mirar, notar)
   Ud. lo mira notando la ropa sucia.

9. The mother looks for her child, calling his name. (buscar, llamar)
   La madre busca a su niño, llamando su nombre.

Remember: **The present participle functions in the above sentences as an adverb, to describe how the true action is performed.**

Read the following sentences to determine how the English gerund (which functions as a noun) is expressed in Spanish.

1. No puedo concentrar a causa del **cantar** de los pájaros.
   *I can't concentrate because of the **singing** of the birds.*

2. **Nadar** es mi deporte favorito.
   ***Swimming** is my favorite sport.*

3. **Robar** es malo.
   ***Stealing** is bad.*

The English gerunds (nouns) are expressed in Spanish <u>*by the infinitive.*</u>

Fill in the blanks with a Spanish infinitive.

3.6 a. He doesn't like reading.

   No le gusta _____ .

b. Working there is difficult.

   _____ allí es difícil.

c. Studying is necessary to pass the exams.

   _____ es necesario para tener éxito en los exámenes.

d. Playing sports is more fun than watching TV.

   _____ a los deportes es más divertido que _____ la televisión.

e. Playing a musical instrument requires practice.

   _____ un instrumento musical requiere la práctica.

f. Smoking is prohibited.

   Se prohibe _____ .

g. Saving money is a good idea.

   _____ el dinero es buena idea.

h. Talking on the phone is our favorite hobby.

   _____ por teléfono es nuestro pasatiempo favorito.

i. We don't like skiing.

   No nos gusta _____ .

j. Climbing mountains is dangerous.

   _____ montañas es peligroso.

Remember: **The present participle (*-ando, -iendo*) may be used as an adverb in Spanish sentences, but the infinitive is used as a gerund, or noun, in Spanish sentences.**

 Choose and circle the verb form (infinitive or present participle) that correctly completes each translation.

3.7   a.   He is reading a novel.

Está (leer, **leyendo**) una novela.

b.   He continues speaking French.

Continúa (hablar, **hablando**) francés.

c.   The child goes to school, crying.

El niño va (llorar, **llorando**) a la escuela.

d.   Reading with the lights off is bad for the eyes.

(**Leer**, Leyendo) con las luces apagadas es malo para los ojos.

e.   Choosing good friends is important.

(**Escoger**, Escogiendo) buenos amigos es importante.

f.   I am not enjoying myself much.

No me estoy (divertir, **divirtiendo**) mucho.

g.   Is he bothering you?

¿Está (molestarte, **molestándote**)?

h.   Eating fruits and vegetables helps you to be healthy.

(**Comer**, Comiendo) las frutas y los vegetales te ayuda a tener buena salud.

i.   You walk, tripping on your shoelace.

Caminas (tropezar, **tropezando**) en el cordón del zapato.

THE EXPRESSION "UPON" (+ INFINITIVE)

Look at the following sample sentence.

| Al oír la mala noticia, ella lloró. | Upon hearing the bad news, she wept. |

Use the idiom *al* + **infinitive** to express the (English) gerund in this structure, because the gerund is functioning as a noun.

When the gerund is used as a noun in a sentence, you use the infinitive of the Spanish verb.

Translate into English.

3.8
a. Al saludar a su amigo, dijo: «¿Cómo estás?»

b. Al saltar del tren, se fracturó la pierna.

c. Al ponerse el vestido, se sintió como princesa.

d. Al cumplir la tarea, estuve contento.

e. Comencé a trabajar al oír la campana (bell).

f. Al ver el oso (bear), corrió muy rápidamente.

g. Te diste cuenta de (You realized) que te olvidaste de peinarte al mirarte en el espejo.

h. Al recibir la leche, el bebé se calmó.

i. Ellos abrieron los regalos al recibirlos.

j. Al acostarnos, nos dormimos.

✓ Adult check _____
                    Initial   Date

Read the passage once to determine the overall meaning of the text. Read it a second time in order to determine, then circle, which verb form, the infinitive or the present participle, is needed.

3.9   El estudiante se está __(1)__ (behaving) nerviosamente. No se está __(2)__ en el examen. Los ojos están __(3)__. Al __(4)__ esto, la profesora se levanta. Se acerca, __(5)__ cuidadosamente. Puede ver que está __(6)__ las respuestas del otro estudiante. __(7)__ es un asunto muy serio en la clase. La profesora quita el examen, __(8)__ que va a llamar a los padres del primer estudiante. Al __(9)__ esto, se siente avergonzado (ashamed). Para él, __(10)__ a los padres es terrible. Van a castigarlo.

1. portar, portando
2. concentrar, concentrando
3. moverse, moviéndose
4. notar, notando
5. estudiarlo, estudiándolo
6. copiar, copiando
7. Copiar, Copiando
8. decir, diciendo
9. oír, oyendo
10. llamar, llamando

Read the passage once to determine the overall meaning of the text. Read it a second time in order to determine, then circle, which verb form, the infinitive or the present participle, is needed.

3.10 El policía está __(1)__ el tráfico. Aunque hace frío y nieva, le gusta __(2)__ porque le gusta __(3)__ afuera. De pronto ve que un camión viene muy rápidamente hacia (towards) un grupo de peatones (pedestrians). El chófer (driver) está __(4)__ control sobre el hielo. Está __(5)__ la bocina (horn) para llamar la atención a las personas. Al __(6)__ la bocina y al __(7)__ el camión, las personas del grupo saltan rápidamente hacia la acera. El camión pasa sin __(8)__ con ellos. Todo está bien.

1. dirigir, dirigiendo
2. dirigirlo, dirigiéndolo
3. estar, estando
4. perder, perdiendo
5. sonar, sonando
6. oír, oyendo
7. ver, viendo
8. chocar, chocando

Fill in the blanks with the infinitive or present participle in order to express the English gerund correctly.

3.11
a. I am receiving candy for my birthday, but I like receiving flowers more.
Yo estoy _____ los dulces para mi cumpleaños, pero me gusta más _____ las flores.

b. Usually, running is his favorite hobby, but now he goes to class running, because he often arrives late. Normalmente _____ es su pasatiempo favorito, pero ahora va a la clase _____ , porque llega tarde muchas veces.

c. Listening to the news is depressing. I'm not listening to the news now.
_____ las noticias es deprimido. No estoy _____ las noticias ahora.

d. She enters the room praying. Praying makes her feel better.
Entra en el cuarto _____ . _____ le hace sentirse mejor.

e. We ride the roller coaster screaming. Not screaming is impossible.
Montamos la montaña rusa _____ . No _____ es imposible.

f. Doing chores is important, although many people aren't doing chores during the weekend.
_____ los quehaceres es importante, aunque muchas personas no están _____ los quehaceres durante el fin de semana.

g. Upon seeing her old friend, she thought she was seeing a ghost.
_____ a su viejo amigo, pensó que estaba _____ un fantasma.

h. Growing roses is a lot of work, but he enjoys growing flowers.
_____ las rosas es mucho trabajo, pero se divierte _____ las flores.

i. Upon choosing that company, she is also choosing how much money she is going to make.
_____ esa compañía, también está _____ cuanto dinero va a ganar.

j. The teacher continues speaking to the students, even though others are still speaking.
El profesor continúa _____ a los estudiantes, aunque otros todavía están _____ .

Speaking

 Imagine you are shopping at a local department store. You are the parent of school-age children and you need to buy school clothes and supplies for them. A salesclerk helps you. **Read the following conversation in English. Work out the conversation, translating it into Spanish with a partner. Write out the dialog and practice orally with your partner.** However, when you are ready to present your conversation, use only an index card with verbs/infinitives written on the card. This will provide good practice for creating the language in your head on the spot.

3.12

el/la dependiente: Are you looking for clothes for children?

el padre/la madre: Yes, they are going to start school next week. I came to shop here because of your reduced prices this week.

el/la dependiente: Children do like new clothes for school.

el padre/la madre: Yes, but I don't like spending too much (*demasiado*) money.

el/la dependiente: It is difficult to find good clothes at inexpensive (*barato*) prices. What do you need for your family?

el padre/la madre: My son always goes out wearing jeans. My daughter likes wearing casual dresses.

el/la dependiente: We have reduced prices on jeans for boys and on dresses for girls.

el padre/la madre: That's wonderful! Where are the jeans for boys?

el/la dependiente: This way.

el/la dependiente: _____

el padre/la madre: _____
_____

el/la dependiente: _____

el padre/la madre: _____

el/la dependiente: _____
_____

el padre/la madre: _____
_____

el/la dependiente: _____
_____

el padre/la madre: _____
_____

el/la dependiente: _____

✓ Adult check _____
            Initial   Date

LISTENING EXERCISES III

Exercise 1. Circle the appropriate Spanish expression of the English gerund that you hear in each phrase: the infinitive or the present participle. [CD–C, Track 7]

a. infinitive   present participle
b. infinitive   present participle
c. infinitive   present participle
d. infinitive   present participle
e. infinitive   present participle
f. infinitive   present participle
g. infinitive   present participle
h. infinitive   present participle
i. infinitive   present participle
j. infinitive   present participle

Exercise 2. Complete the phrase by choosing and circling the correct verb form (the infinitive or the present participle). [CD–C, Track 8]

a. (levantarnos, levantándonos) la mano.
b. (recibir, recibiendo) las malas noticias.
c. (huir, huyendo) del peligro.
d. (tratar, tratando) de hablar claramente.
e. (estudiar, estudiando) es imposible.
f. (rogarle, rogándole) la ayuda.
g. (recibira, recibiendo) la cuenta.
h. (ganar, ganando) la lotería.
i. (terminar, terminando) la tarea.
j. (caminar, caminando) a casa.

Exercise 3. Decide how to rewrite the phrases you hear with one of the following expressions: an infinitive, *al* + infinitive, or a present participial phrase. Conjugate the verbs where necessary. [CD–C, Track 9]

a. _____

b. _____

c. _____

d. _____

e. _____

✔ Adult check _____
                           Initial   Date

 Review the material in this section in preparation for the Self Test. This Self Test will check your mastery of this particular section as well as your knowledge of the previous sections.

SELF TEST 3

3.01 **Give the present participle of the following verbs.** (2 pts. each)

a. leer _____   f. preferir _____

b. dormir _____   g. aprender _____

c. estudiar _____   h. huir _____

d. pedir _____   i. creer _____

e. traer _____   j. escribir _____

3.02 **Choose the correct form of the verb.** (1 pt. each)

a. Al (estudiar / estudiando) mucho, podía tener éxito en el examen.

b. Corrimos (llorar / llorando) de la casa.

c. El profesor está (hablar / hablando) inglés.

d. No me gusta (comer / comiendo) demasiado por la noche.

e. Fuiste a la clase (gritar / gritando) el nombre de tu amigo.

f. (Jugar / Jugando) en el equipo de béisbol requiere mucho tiempo.

g. Es necesario (hablar / hablando) por teléfono cuando se trabaja en una oficina.

h. Ellos no se están (sentar / sentando) en los sillones verdes.

i. Al (terminar / terminando) la tarea, sacó una buena nota.

j. (Vestirse / Vistiéndose) bien es importante para una ocasión formal.

3.03 **Fill in the blank with the correct Spanish word.** (2 pts. each)

a. Se prohibe _____ (smoking).

b. No te gusta _____ (cooking).

c. _____ (Studying) en la biblioteca es necesario.

d. _____ (Talking) por teléfono es mi pasatiempo favorito.

e. _____ (Feeling) triste, yo lloro por veinte minutos.

f. Miro la película, _____ (noting—notar) el vestido bonito de la actriz.

g. Conduce el coche, _____ (looking for) la casa de Raúl.

h. _____ (Leaving) temprano no es una idea muy buena.

i. Al _____ (setting) la mesa, no pudo encontrar los tenedores.

j. Caminamos por el parque _____ (enjoying ourselves, having a good time).

40 / 50

Score _____

Adult check _____
    Initial   Date

IV. GRAMMAR REVIEW: UNIT THREE

Decide if the following sentences were isolated incidents or habitual actions of the past. Fill in the blanks with preterit forms for the isolated actions and imperfect forms for the habitual.

4.1
   a. El año pasado tú _____ en España. (vivir)

   b. Yo _____ tres días estudiando para el examen de matemáticas. (pasar)

   c. Los jueves Uds. _____ a la clase de español. (ir)

   d. Ayer yo _____ con mi mejor amigo. (charlar)

   e. Muchas veces nosotros _____ a nuestros hermanos menores. (ayudar)

   f. Durante aquella época la gente _____ la ropa elegante. (llevar)

   g. Durante su niñez Uds. _____ muchos amigos. (tener)

   h. Juan la _____ dos veces. (ver)

   i. ¿Quiénes _____ el museo el sábado pasado? (visitar)

   j. Todos los lunes nosotros _____ a las clases. (asistir)

Rewrite the sentences in the past tense. You will have to choose between the imperfect tense for background/descriptive action and the preterit tense for simple action.

4.2
   a. No vamos porque llueve.
_____

   b. Son las dos y media cuando salimos.
_____

   c. ¿Nieva cuando te despiertas?
_____

   d. La mujer que se cae lleva una falda gris.
_____

   e. Me dan una fiesta cuando tengo seis años.
_____

   f. Es el once de octubre. Sacas una mala nota en el examen de ciencias.
_____
_____

g. ¿Qué tiempo hace cuando están de vacaciones?
_____

h. Son las once de la noche cuando termino la tarea.
_____

i. El chico que lleva un short blanco y una camiseta verde juega al béisbol muy bien hoy.
_____

j. El chico de quien hablo es pelirrojo.
_____

Each sentence in this exercise illustrates an interrupted action and a simple, completed action (in English). Fill in an imperfect form and a preterit form in order to complete each sentence.

4.3
a. I was listening to the radio when the telephone rang.

_____ la radio cuando _____ el teléfono.

b. Mariel was talking to him when I interrupted them.

Mariel le _____ cuando yo los _____ .

c. At the moment we said good-bye, she wasn't listening to me.

Al momento en que nos _____ , ella no me _____ .

d. You threw (echar) the ball while I wasn't looking at you.

Tú _____ la pelota cuando no te _____ .

e. Wasn't he going out with her when she got sick?

¿No _____ con ella cuando se _____ ?

f. My dad bought the car when its price was reduced.

Mi padre _____ el coche cuando su precio _____ rebajado.

g. Who ate the cookie I had in the fridge?

¿Quién _____ la galleta que _____ en el refrigerador?

h. I was walking through the park when suddenly I saw my aunt.

_____ por el parque cuando de repente _____ a mi tía.

i. While we were watching the movie, the lights turned off.

Mientras _____ la película, se _____ las luces.

j. My pencil broke while I was taking the test.

Mi lápiz se _____ mientras _____ el examen.

The imperfect tense often describes mental activity while the preterit expresses physical action. Circle the appropriate verb tense forms to complete each sentence.

4.4 a. (Estaba / Estuvo) contenta porque (estaba / estuvo) con su mejor amigo.

b. Me (alegraba / alegré) porque (contestaba / contesté) a la pregunta correctamente.

c. Ellos (corrían / corrieron) a la escuela ayer porque no (querían / quisieron) llegar tarde.

d. ¿Qué (pensaba / pensó) Ud. de los eventos que (ocurrían / ocurrieron) ayer?

e. No lo (creía / creyó) nunca.

f. Una mosca se (caía / cayó) en mi sopa. No (quería / quise) comer más.

g. Ud. se (presentaba / presentó) muy bien ayer. (Parecía / Pareció) muy inteligente.

h. Tú (estabas / estuviste) orgullosa porque tu hijo (ganaba / ganó) el premio.

i. Nosotros (pensábamos / pensamos) en la respuesta correcta cuando (levantábamos / levantamos) la mano.

j. Él (escogía / escogió) el abrigo que (quería / quiso) comprar.

Would you use *por* or *para* if you were translating these sentences? Decide which preposition would replace the *italicized* word. Write your choice in the space provided.

4.5 a. _____ *By* coming home late, he got into a lot of trouble.

b. _____ She sent the letter *by* plane from New York to London.

c. _____ I need the book *in order* to do the homework.

d. _____ We drove *for* eight hours.

e. _____ She has the tickets *for* tomorrow.

f. _____ That house was built *by* my father.

g. _____ You need your dress cleaned *for* the party tomorrow night.

h. _____ Those cookies aren't *for* you!

i. _____ I have to work *for* Enrique today, because he's sick.

j. _____ We work *for* a large company.

Fill in the blank with the correct word or phrase: *pero, sino,* **or** *sino que.*

4.6
a. Intentaba asistir a tu fiesta, _____ al fin, no podía.

b. No estudia el francés, _____ el español.

c. Quiero visitar a mi amiga en California, _____ no me gusta viajar en avión.

d. No hablas por teléfono con él, _____ escríbelo una carta.

e. No bebemos el té, _____ el café.

f. Busco cincuenta centavos en la bolsa, _____ no puedo encontrar ningún dinero en ninguna parte.

g. Tu chaqueta no está en el armario, _____ está en el suelo de tu dormitorio.

h. Jugué al tenis con los muchachos, _____ quería ir al cine.

i. ¿Sabías lo qué hicieron, _____ no dijiste nada a nadie?

j. No mienta (lie) al policía, _____ dígale la verdad.

Below is a list of different excuses some students gave for not completing an assignment. Decide which word or phrase, *a causa de* **or** *porque,* **would complete each excuse.**

4.7   No hice mi tarea...

a. _____ mi perro la comió.

b. _____ la tormenta.

c. _____ no tuve suficiente tiempo.

d. _____ las luces apagadas.

e. _____ no entendí nada.

f. _____ la perdí.

g. _____ una muerte dentro de la familia.

h. _____ se murió mi tío.

i. _____ una enfermedad grave.

j. _____ otras tareas muy importantes.

Decide which word or phrase would be used in each translation: *por, para, a causa de, porque, pero, sino, sino que.*

4.8
a. I meant to read for only an hour, but I couldn't stop reading it.

   Pensaba leer _____ solamente una hora, _____ no podía dejar de leerlo.

b. It's because of his illness he is so weak.

   Es _____ su enfermedad que es tan débil.

c. We didn't go to the library, but to Raul's house.

   No fuimos a la biblioteca, _____ a la casa de Raúl.

d. You have to return the magazine by Saturday.

   Tienes que devolver la revista _____ el sábado.

e. We love ice cream, but we eat very little.

   Nos encanta el helado, _____ comemos muy poco.

f. She didn't go to the party last night, because she had to work.

   Ella no fue a la fiesta anoche, _____ tuvo que trabajar.

g. They didn't order steak, but salads.

   No pidieron el bistec, _____ las ensaladas.

h. In order to get home on time, you had to take the bus.

   _____ llegar a casa a tiempo, Uds. tuvieron que tomar el autobús.

i. You couldn't drive because of the storm.

   No pudiste conducir _____ la tormenta.

j. Do you need the tools to fix your bike?

   ¿Necesita Ud. las herramientas _____ reparar su bicicleta?

Decide if the following items belong logically in the location given. Write *sí* if the pairing is commonly logical. Write *no* otherwise, and correctly name the place most commonly associated with that item.

4.9
a. las herramientas/la cocina _____
b. el sofá/la sala _____
c. la cama/el dormitorio _____
d. la bañera/el comedor _____
e. el fregadero/el jardín _____
f. la olla/la cocina _____
g. los tenedores/el garaje _____
h. un sillón/el comedor _____
i. la manguera/el jardín _____
j. el espejo/el garaje _____
k. los gabinetes/el dormitorio _____
l. la ducha/el baño _____
m. el refrigerador/el comedor _____
n. el lavabo/la cocina _____
o. la almohada/el garaje _____

In Spanish, name the item described. Include the definite article with each term.

4.10 a. donde se sienta _____

b. una cosa para dar el agua a las plantas _____

c. una cosa para comunicar _____

d. donde se ponen las cucharas, los tenedores y los cuchillos _____

e. la cosa que cubre el suelo _____

f. lo que se usa para cocinar rápidamente _____

g. donde se pone la ropa _____

h. en qué te miras _____

i. de qué bebes _____

j. las que se usan para decorar las ventanas _____

k. una mesa pequeña al lado de la cama _____

l. la cosa para limpiar la alfombra _____

m. una silla muy grande y cómoda _____

n. en que se cocinan los huevos _____

o. donde duermes _____

✓ Adult check _____
                         Initial   Date

 Describe the picture below. Mention what furniture is present. Describe the furniture. Describe what the people are doing and what they are using. Write ten complete Spanish sentences.

4.11

✓ Adult check _____
                    Initial   Date

Speaking

 Improve your spoken Spanish. Take turns discussing the items pictured. Discuss and describe them, using a variety of vocabulary words you have learned.

4.12

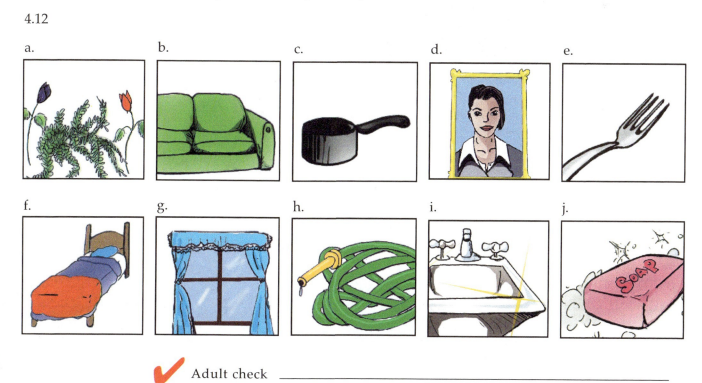

✓ Adult check _____
                    Initial   Date

Write a story in Spanish about the picture below. Use the preterit and the imperfect verb tenses. Your story must NOT be merely descriptive, and you may NOT use dialogue of any sort. You must relate the action of the picture. You may choose to include the characters' feelings and desires. You may wish to discuss reasons for the characters' actions. You may wish to discuss what happened after the events of the picture.

4.13

Adult check _____ _____
                        Initial   Date

V. CULTURE: SPAIN

Map Study. Review the geography of Spain. Use an atlas and your map studies from Unit One to label the map. Include the following points of interest.

5.1 Important cities:

1. Madrid
2. Santiago de Compostela
3. Bilbao
4. Vigo
5. Segovia
6. Burgos
7. Toledo
8. Córdoba
9. Cartagena
10. Pamplona
11. Barcelona
12. Sevilla
13. Granada
14. Salamanca
15. Oviedo
16. Mérida
17. Santander
18. Zaragosa

Topographical features:

19. the Strait of Gibraltar
20. the Atlantic Ocean
21. the Mediterranean Sea
22. the Balearic Islands
23. the Bay of Biscay
24. the Pyrenees Mountains
25. the Sierra Nevada Mountains
26. Portugal
27. the Guadalquivir River
28. the Ebro River
29. the Duero River
30. the Guadiana River
31. France

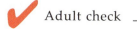 Adult check _____
   Initial   Date

Spain is politically divided into numerous provinces. Although each province considers itself culturally unique and truly is politically autonomous (from one another), historically, they have been categorized into fifteen major regions. Review the map below.

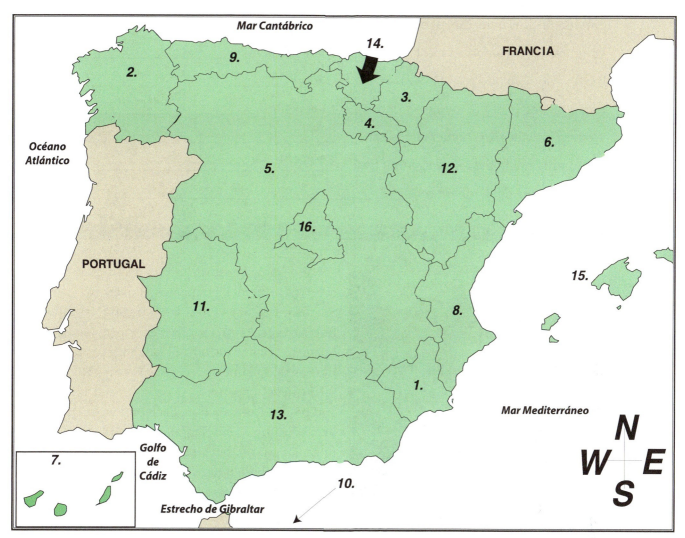

 Label the blank map with the fifteen provinces presented in this chapter.

5.2
a. _____ Extremadura
b. _____ La Rioja
c. _____ Asturias
d. _____ Valencia
e. _____ las Islas Baleares
f. _____ Murcia
g. _____ Ceuta y Melilla
h. _____ Galicia

i. _____ Andalucía
j. _____ Cataluña
k. _____ Navarra
l. _____ el País Vasco
m. _____ las Islas Canarias
n. _____ Castilla y León/Castilla-La Mancha
o. _____ Aragón
p. _____ Madrid

✔ Adult check _____
  Initial   Date

 Name the Spanish province described.

5.3
1. Island province off the northwest coast of Africa _____

2. Province located directly north of Portugal _____

3. Two Moroccan port cities held by Spain _____

79

4. Province in which the capital city is located _____

5. Province which comprises most of the central area of Spain _____

6. Province located next to el País Vasco and La Rioja _____

7. Province located at the southeastern corner of the peninsula _____

8. Western province that borders Portugal _____

9. Island province in the Mediterranean Sea _____

10. Province along the northern coast _____

You may be surprised to learn that there are fourteen different languages spoken in Spain. The Spanish language you are learning is called (by English speakers) *Castilian* Spanish. *Castellano* (in Spanish) became the official language of Spain during the Fascist Regime of Francisco Franco. The people of Spain have long resented being forced into cultural and political assimilation. Each province clings tightly to its cultural and language identity. Historically, these languages have been grouped into five major regions. Although *castellano* is spoken throughout the country, a traveler is as likely to hear any of the fourteen languages spoken today.

 Review the map to decide where these languages are spoken in Spain. Use the list of cities from the second map activity. Study the list of cities under each language.

5.4

andaluz	castellano	vasco/vascuence/euskara	catalán	gallego
Sevilla	Segovia	Bilbao	Barcelona	Santiago de Compostela
Granada	Madrid	San Sebastián	Islas Baleares	Vigo
Córdoba	Salamanca			La Coruña
Málaga	Toledo			

✔ Adult check _____
                    Initial   Date

Now answer the questions in complete Spanish sentences.

1. ¿Dónde se habla catalán?
   _____

2. ¿Dónde se habla gallego?
   _____

3. ¿Dónde se habla castellano?
   _____

4. ¿Dónde se habla andaluz?
   _____

5. ¿Dónde se habla vasco?
   _____

Create your own map detailing the different regions of language. Your map should be full color. Color code each language to an accompanying key. The names of each language should be listed in the key.

5.5

✓ Adult check _____
                    Initial   Date

Optional Activity. See the Answer Key.

Before you take the LIFEPAC Test, you may want to do one or more of these self checks.
1. _____ Read the objectives. Determine if you can do them.
2. _____ Restudy the material related to any objectives that you cannot do.
3. _____ Use the SQ3R study procedure to review the material.
4. _____ Review all activities, Self Tests, and LIFEPAC vocabulary words.
5. _____ Restudy areas of weakness indicated by the last Self Test.

VOCABULARY LIST
[CD–C, Track 13]

NOUNS

el abrigo – the overcoat
el anillo – the ring
el arete – the (post) earring
la billetera – the wallet
la blusa – the blouse
la bolsa – the purse, bag
la bota – the boot
la bufanda – the scarf
los caballeros – the men
la cadena – the chain
la cadena de oro – the gold chain
la cadena de plata – the silver chain
el calcetín – the sock
la calidad – the quality
la camisa – the (button-down) shirt
la camiseta – the T-shirt
la cantidad – the quantity
la cartera – the wallet
la chaqueta – the jacket
la chaqueta sudadera – the sweatshirt
el cinturón – the belt
el collar – the necklace
los complementos – the accessories
la corbata – the tie
el cuero – the leather
las damas – the ladies
el descuento – the discount
el diamante – the diamond
la falda – the skirt
la foto – the photo
la gorra – the cap, baseball hat
los guantes – the gloves
el impermeable – the raincoat
los jeans – the jeans
las joyas – the jewels, jewelry
las medias – the stockings
la mochila – the backpack
la mujer – the woman
el número – the size (shoes, gloves)
los pantalones – the pants
los pantalones cortos – the shorts
un par – a pair
el paraguas – the umbrella
el pendiente – the drop (dangle) earring
los pijamas – the pajamas
el precio – the price
los precios a partir de… – prices starting at . . .
los precios rebajados – reduced prices
la pulsera – the bracelet
la ropa – the clothing, clothes
la ropa deportiva – the sports clothing
la ropa interior para caballeros (para hombres) – the men's underwear
la ropa interior para damas (para mujeres) – the ladies' underwear
la seda – the silk
el short – the (pair of) shorts
el sombrero – the hat
el suéter – the sweater
la talla – the size (dress, shirt, etc.)
la tarjeta de crédito – the credit card
la tela – the fabric
los tenis – the tennis shoes, sneakers
el traje – the suit
el traje de baño – the bathing suit, swimsuit
los vaqueros – the jeans
el vestido – the dress
los vestidos – the clothes
el zapatillo – the slipper
el zapato – the shoe
los zapatos de tacones altos – the high-heeled shoes, high heels
los zapatos de tacones bajos – the low heeled-shoes, flats
los zapatos de tenis – the tennis shoes, sneakers

VERBS

aumentar – to increase
colgar (o-ue) – to hang (up)
comprar – to buy
conseguir (e-i) – to get
deber – to owe; should, must (with an infinitive)
llevar – to wear, carry
obtener – to obtain, get
ponerse – to put on (clothing)
probarse (o-ue) – to try on (clothing)
quitarse – to take off (clothing)
tener – to have
tener que – to have to, must (with an infinitive)
traer – to bring
vestirse – to get dressed

ADJECTIVES

ancho – wide
apretado – tight
arrugado – wrinkled
barato – inexpensive, cheap (in price)
bonito – pretty
caro – expensive
claro – bright; light (color)
cómodo – comfortable
corto – short
elegante – elegant, dressy
estrecho – narrow
feo – ugly
fino – fine
flojo – loose-fitting
formal – formal
grande – big, large
informal – informal, casual
largo – long
limpio – clean
mediano – medium
mojado – wet
nuevo – new
oscuro – dark (color)
pequeño – small, little
suave – smooth
sucio – dirty
suficiente – enough
viejo – old

ADVERBS

bastante – rather, very, quite, enough
muy – very
seguramente – safely, securely
tan – so (+ adjective)